THE END OF ARROGANCE

THE END OF
ARROGANCE

America in the Global Competition of Ideas

STEVEN WEBER
BRUCE W. JENTLESON

HARVARD UNIVERSITY PRESS
Cambridge, Massachusetts, and London, England
2010

Library of Congress Cataloging-in-Publication Data
Weber, Steven.
The end of arrogance : America in the global competition of ideas /
Steven Weber and Bruce W. Jentleson.
p. cm.
Includes bibliographical references and index.
ISBN 978-0-674-05818-7 (alk. paper)
1. Labor market—History—21st century. 2. Technological innovations—
21st century. 3. Globalization—21st century. 4. Emigration and
immigration—21st century. I. Jentleson, Bruce W. II. Title.
HD5706.W39 2010
327.73—dc22   2010026398

To mentors, colleagues, students

CONTENTS

Preface   ix

1. Big Open Questions   1
2. A Global Competition of Ideas   17
3. Forging a Just Society   61
4. Pursuing a Twenty-First-Century World Order   101
5. Being Strategic about the Future   148

Notes   197
Index   204

PREFACE

All the talk in the wake of 9-11 about the "war" of ideas just didn't click with us. Ideas fighting wars: what does that look like? And should it have been defined so neatly as freedom versus fundamentalism at a time when so much else was in flux amid the ramifications of the end of the Cold War and the dynamics of globalization?

We felt that what all that talk did get right was the focus on ideas. Ideas matter. They always have, and they do especially now. It is our view that world politics has entered a new and distinctive age in which ideas and influence are linked in a vibrant and sometimes ferocious competition for ascendance. Core questions about how best to achieve world order and what constitutes just societies, seemingly settled at the end of the twentieth century, have been reopened in the twenty-first century. Yet America's position in this global competition of ideas is less robust than most Americans think—and weaker than we need.

Our sense was that neither aspect of this international landscape was being sufficiently recognized. Not by liberals who over-attributed the problems to George W. Bush and the solutions to retapping pre-Bush styles of global leadership. Nor by neoconservatives who were more dismissive of the critique and more assertive of what America could and should do. More fundamentally, we saw across the political spectrum a shared sense that America would still provide the ideological leadership the world needed, and that aside from some outliers, that was what the world wanted.

That's the arrogance that concerns us. Arrogance in a policy context is not a problem because feelings get hurt. It is a problem because it is a disposition counterproductive to competing effectively in this twenty-first-century global marketplace of ideas. Arrogance, as we use it in the title, refers to policies, not people. Arrogant policies carry with them a strong sense of entitlement—an embedded belief that others should listen, understand, agree (more or less), and act in ways that the policies suggest. When arrogance fades, real and meaningful influence grows.

Developing such new strategies is not only a foreign policy problem for those in Washington, but a business model problem for global corporations, philanthropies, and nongovernmental organizations that operate on a world stage. The global competition among ideas is much more a buyer's market than a seller's market, because leaders need followers more than the other way around.

And it is relentlessly energetic. This is a market that incessantly breeds new contenders, because barriers to entry are so much lower for ideological competition than for military or economic competition.

While it is powerful to look *inward* at traditional American values for guidance about what to do next, it is not powerful to look *backward* at what may have worked in the past, when the competition took different forms and was much less vibrant. A future leadership proposition has to be *adaptive, not restorative;* looking forward, not backward; and most important, it has to be designed first and foremost to appeal to the needs of the people abroad whose allegiance it is seeking to gain—not the people at home who want to feel good about their presence in the world.

We offer in this book a forward-looking leadership proposition that we believe can compete successfully in today's (and tomorrow's) global marketplace of ideas. The core ingredients are these: A strategy for world order that rests on mutuality, recognizing that in twenty-first-century world politics everyone bargains with everyone and no one is entitled to set the rules. A framework for just societies that better balances individual and societal rights, recognizing that in many global settings the legitimacy of institutions depends on their performance in meeting human needs as much or more than the processes they embed. And, all told, a vision for the future that inspires others with purpose, not just power; that positions not just America but anyone who wants to come with us for a decent shot at the primary global challenge: Can the lives of 7 or 8 billion people be improved without poisoning the planet and killing each other over energy, water, food, and ultimately the terms of human dignity?

When arrogance fades, the need to make hard choices among things we want and allocate our efforts accordingly comes into focus. This too is an opportunity, because it is in the act of making hard choices that presumptive leaders demonstrate to the market, in unequivocal and powerful ways, what their ideas and values truly represent. Real leaders don't hide from gut-wrenching choices and hope they will go away—they lean into them and set the terms by which others then choose. And so the final chapter of this book explains what it means to act strategically in this new world. This is where policy demonstrates what we stand for, not just what we say, and where the visible connections between rhetoric and reality are constantly tested by an audience that is global, technologically empowered, skeptical, and restless for change.

We have made a conscious decision in writing this book to leave out most of the short-term items on the American foreign policy agenda, as critical as those are. In our view there is simply no choice between dealing with today's crises and dealing with the longer-term global competition of ideas; it has to be both/and not either/or. We understand and are deeply sympathetic to the urgencies of government and corporate decision making, but we've yet to meet a strategist in either setting who is fully satisfied with the existing balance. We hope the arguments in this book contribute to the both/and, and to a better balance between them, by providing some real options that decision makers can use to both short-term and longer-term advantage.

We have also made a conscious effort to get beyond partisan arguments. There are probably points in this book that will invigorate and infuriate Republicans and Democrats, liberals and conservatives, and beyond. That's okay with us, if our prompting and provocations lead to better and more relevant disagreements that in turn contribute to effective decisions and policies.

We have had a great deal of help and support in the discussions, arguments, and everything that led us to write this book. Our article "America's Hard Sell," the cover story in *Foreign Policy* 169 (Nov./Dec. 2008), was an initial opportunity to lay out some of our main arguments. We were pleased to be featured in a publication known for its innovative approach to global affairs, and are grateful to *Foreign Policy* editors and other staff.

The Carnegie Corporation of New York has generously supported our work on this book as well as related initiatives. Our appreciation to Vartan Gregorian, and especially to Stephen Del Rosso for his colleagueship well beyond his formal foundation responsibilities. His ideas and insights have been of great intellectual and substantive value. We have also received support from the Rockefeller Brothers Fund, for which we thank Stephen Heintz and Priscilla Lewis, and from Duke University and the University of California, Berkeley. We've benefited enormously from an ongoing dialogue with an extraordinary group of colleagues including but not limited to

Naazneen Barma, Michael Barnett, Regina Connell, Brent Durbin, Alan Kantrow, Parag Khanna, Matthew Kroenig, Eric Lorber, Karen Monaghan, Jay Okey, Ely Ratner, and Janice Stein. Our friends at the Monitor Group and particularly Monitor 360 have kept us up at night by relentlessly asking hard questions. Marie Aberger, Sara Huff, Rachel Wald, and Jessica Wirth have provided valuable research assistance; Susan Alexander, David Arrington, Belinda Keith, and Jessie Owen have provided valuable staff assistance.

We dedicate this book to our mentors with thanks for their guidance, colleagues from whom we've gained much, and students who continue to inspire.

I

BIG OPEN QUESTIONS

Five big ideas shaped world politics in the twentieth century:

Peace was better than war.

Hegemony, at least the benign sort, was better than balance of power.

Capitalism was better than socialism.

Democracy was better than dictatorship.

Western culture was better than all the rest.

On all five counts, the United States was widely seen as paragon and guarantor. American power brought peace through a combination of Cold War containment and deterrence, a United Nations based largely on American design, and U.S.-buttressed European unity. It was American hegemony—"benign hegemony" we called it—that brought relative security and progressively more open trade and capital markets, explained as beneficial by

American development theory. American capitalism taught the world how to create unprecedented wealth as well as how to discover and deploy incredible technology. American democracy inspired publics around the world to upgrade their relationships with political authority. And with all its idiosyncrasies, American culture became a magnet in particular for much of the world's youth.

As we have moved into the twenty-first century, the prevailing consensus inside the United States is that these five big ideas carry over as the basis for present and future world order. There have been a variety of formulations—the end of history, the democratic peace, the indispensable nation, the Rome-like empire, a flat world—which despite their differences share the core belief that the fundamentals have not changed. Even the latest spate of slightly anxious books about the "second" or "post-American" world end up in this same place.[1] There are and will be other important actors on the world stage, these books argue. But those actors are still said to be reading from basically the same script. The players are doing some shifting, some structures and institutions need refurbishing—but though power and wealth will be rebalanced, there is no indication in these books that core ideologies will be reexamined and reopened. The big ideas, many think, still form the foundation for present and future international politics.

We're not so sure. The five big ideas of the last century are no longer the sound and sturdy guides they once were. That is why the challenge of leadership runs far deeper than the atmospherics created by any particular policy or administration. And that is why today's international institutions are not simply in need of remodeling and refurbishing to reflect shifts in power and wealth across the globe. The rules have changed, and the biggest, most basic questions of world politics are now open for debate.

Consider the first big idea: "Peace is better than war." Of course it is when you like the status quo. If you don't, war is consistently wielded as an instrument of national policy—as was the case with the United States in Iraq and Afghanistan, Russia in Georgia, Ethiopia in Somalia, Israel in Lebanon, and lots of others to come. That's not a new thing. Now consider the supposed superiority of peace in light of the desire of at least some global actors to prevent the killing of civilians in Darfur, or to end the malign neglect in the aftermath of natural disaster in Burma, or to head off a pandemic incubating within sovereign borders. With authority more contested and power more diffuse, what are the rules for going to war and keeping the peace?

Further, who makes them? Hegemony (benign or otherwise) is no longer an option—not for the United States, not for China, not for anyone else. A twenty-first-century version of a nineteenth-century multipolar world is hardly possible either. This is no longer an 1800s-style game played among five sovereign states with shared religions, cultures, educational traditions, and intermarried royal families. Too many players sit at too many tables to allow for the counting and balancing of poles of power. More players and players of more types matter more deeply than ever before. Is there a politically relevant distribution of power that doesn't include the Gates Foundation, Google, and Bono—each of which are autonomous global players on the front lines of international politics? Hegemony itself is becoming something of a quaint anachronism, along with traditional stories about the balance of power.

Capitalism, the bulwark of the third big idea, did decisively beat socialism. But capitalism has split into distinctive and, most important, competing forms, with governments owning and directing large and strategic parts of the economies of some of the most critical states and sectors. Consider the core of the energy sector, for example, where, in a radical reversal from fifteen years ago, national oil companies now own more than three-quarters of the world's known oil reserves. Take a look at finance, where openly state-owned banks in some countries now interact with massive financial institutions in others that as "private" institutions were nonetheless bailed out by states, are intimately regulated by states, and whose compensation of executives is overseen by states because they are "too big to fail." Are these really private institutions that respond solely to market signals when allocating capital? Are the negotiations among global money center banks now meaningfully separate from government policy? The "market," whatever it really is, has come to rely on the state as much or more than the state relies on the market.

Democracy has contributed to freer societies. But has democracy proven itself effective in creating just and peaceful ones? That China, the world's most populous nondemocratic state, has had the greatest success meeting the basic human needs of its people and pulling hundreds of millions out of poverty in the past twenty years, presents a massive data point that speaks volumes to this claim. It is hardly a moral acceptance of repression to recognize and acknowledge a factual reality: In many societies political legitimacy is a function of performance, not just process.

Finally, consider culture. President Barack Obama's administration has masterfully reversed some of the most raw and visceral sentiments and expressions of anti-Americanism that were part and parcel of the G. W. Bush years. It will be a long time before another American president can claim an 80 percent increase in popularity over a previous president in a foreign country.[2] But make no mistake: popularity does not equal cultural predominance. The era of imitation, about which some Americans will always wax nostalgic, will not return. Modernization did not bring homogenization of culture in the twentieth century, nor will it in the twenty-first. The short period during which some parts of the world idolized American culture (never as much or as broadly as Americans liked to believe) was a nearly unique historical exception to that rule. Culture and identity are powerful, enduring forces between as much as within societies. How do we live with this heterogeneity, nationally as well as globally?

It's not that these twentieth-century big ideas were wrong. They were largely right for their era. And much about them still rings true. But human and societal progress depend on adaptation to new realities. It is in this sense that these particular ideas have run their historical course. They no longer sufficiently fit the realities people face. The big questions have been reopened—not just at the margins, and not just one at a time. The challenges to the five big ideas of the twentieth century—*when taken together*—create a profoundly different and much more challenging reality. The twenty-first century will not be an ideological rerun of the latter half of the twentieth. Welcome to the new age of ideology.

"Wait a minute," you might say. We're talking about human beings in politics, so what people think and think about surely matters. But in a world filled with very real threats to physical security and welfare, can ideology really matter all that much? There's some scary stuff out there that is not just sitting in people's minds. Global financial crises, swine flu, nuclear proliferation in the Middle East, the illegal narcotics economy, and growing levels of greenhouse gases dominate the media and capture our attention. There's really no getting away from these bad things. They are the outward manifestations of secular trends that wax and wane from year to year but in no case simply go away. And these trends are connected—in some cases interconnected. Tightly coupled complex human systems often *appear* to be quite stable. People tell themselves reassuring stories about how these systems are diversified and robust. And they keep telling those stories up until the moment when they collapse—often catastrophically: modern technology and the 2010 Deepwater Horizon oil spill; modern city planning and Hurricane Katrina in New Orleans; modern finance and the 2008 financial meltdown. There is very little slack in many of the systems, both natural and manmade, on which human beings depend to sustain their lives, economies, and political systems. That's why "tipping points," "black swans," and "tail risks" aren't rare at all. It should no longer be a surprise when so-called small causes have very large effects.[3]

So even though real, concrete problems seem to pile up faster than human beings can deal with them, leaving little time for ideology, in fact ideology is not so easily waylaid. E. H. Carr explained one reason why in his classic 1939 book *The Twenty Years Crisis*.[4] Carr is generally remembered as a skeptic about the importance of ideology in the absence of power, but he was just as much a skeptic about the importance of power in the absence of ideology. It's not lofty rhetoric that makes a difference, but the capacity to define actionable principles of morality and meaning that motivates human beings to act. As Carr eloquently said, the realm of international politics lacks authoritative legal mechanisms for getting to and enforcing agreements. Which means it really is politics, not law, that influences the course of human events from start to finish. And in politics, ideas and ideology are a critical currency.

We should not necessarily expect a particular set of ideas to fill the void, nor should we anticipate that we have finally reached the endpoint of ideology, where human life is simply a pragmatic grab bag, and no one cares from whence a solution comes. Ideas still matter—a lot.

We can't conceive of a world lacking in ideas such as these: the core principles by which societies organize themselves; the rules by which states interact with each other and with their populations; the ways in which knowledge is structured, communicated, shared, and used; and the notion of legitimacy for any kind of political order, at whatever scale, from the authority of the village elder to the weight of a Supreme Court opinion or the power of a United Nations (UN) resolution. Even a claim that something is true or false gets settled most of the time not through objective study but in the realm of ideas. Philosophers with their paradigms, psychologists with their belief systems, and political consultants with their framing all stress the importance of the ideational frameworks within which people interpret and integrate the world around them.

It is because the questions about world politics are both so big and so open that the global competition of ideas is an essential ingredient of international politics, though an uncertain one. That's not a statement that sidesteps the traditional concerns of political realists, military strategists, and hard-headed statesmen and stateswomen. It's an honest recognition that ideological competition is a critical part of the international power politics game.

Some things about national power are relatively certain. Traditional foreign-policy realists think first of military and second of economic capabilities as the key vectors of national power, and they are probably right to do so. The general parameters of military and economic capability for the next decade are foreseeable with a reasonable level of confidence. Barring some extraordinary discontinuity, the United States will in 2020 still be the most capable military power and a predominant center of economic power. Of course there is variance in precisely how those vectors may play out. U.S. military power could decline in important ways relative to China and others, particularly if our current military investments in Iraq, Afghanistan, and Pakistan turn sour. U.S. economic power could be meaningfully hurt if we mismanage our currency, our energy dependence, or the landing (soft or hard) from our massive deficits. But the terrain for these issues is pretty well understood. The U.S. advantage in military and economic power is sufficiently large that the general outcome is robust. It may be impossible to say exactly how far ahead of others the United States is in these areas, but it will still be ahead, and at least in the military realm, probably by quite a lot.

The situation is dramatically less clear when it comes to the ideological components of power. Ideas have become the most uncertain while critically important ingredient of national power calculations. For the United States to compete effectively in that game, government policy must reflect three truths.

It's a Copernican, not a Ptolemaic, world. The ancient philosopher Ptolemy believed Earth was at the center of the universe, with all the other planets, indeed the whole solar system, revolving around it. So too in the dominant twentieth-century view was the United States at the center of the international political world. The United States was the wielder of power in the Cold War, the economic engine driving the international economy, and the bastion of free-world ideology. Indeed, with the demise and defeat of the Soviet Union, American centrality seemed even more assured. The United States was the sole surviving superpower. The American economy was branding globalization. Democracy was spreading the world over. The world at the end of the twentieth century, ironically, seemed even more Ptolemaic.

Not anymore. The twenty-first century is better represented by the discoveries of Copernicus, in which the United States (Earth in the astronomical version) is not at the center. Although our "gravitational pull" is still strong, it is not so strong that others orbit around us. We have seen this geopolitically as other powers have been rising (China), recovering (Russia), maturing (European Union), and emerging (India, Brazil, and others either emerging from a long colonial past or shaking off the lingering effects of superpower dominance). We see it economically every day now. It was the U.S. National Intelligence Council that indicated how globalization is losing its "Made in the USA" character, and it is IBM, the iconic technology company, whose executives choke if you mistakenly call IBM an "American" company. They will remind you continuously that theirs is and always will be a global firm. We see it scientifically as cutting-edge research in green technology, biotechnology, and other frontiers is globally sourced. We see it in so many other walks of life. A New York art dealer, after a recent auction dominated by newly moneyed non-Western collectors, reflected that "for the first time in nearly two hundred years the Western world doesn't make the decisions about our future."[5] Or setting the prices. Or controlling the outcomes. That's the hallmark reality of a Copernican world order.

TINA is not enough. The "there is no alternative" (TINA) argument—that whatever the flaws of a global system led by the United States, there was in practice no substitute—was quite useful for many years. At times it was used cynically. Although it did bear out in some circumstances, in a Copernican world it has much less truth and much less purpose.

Most no longer believe that the alternative to a U.S. world order is chaos. The rules and norms of that order are subject to much more extensive and intensive debate than ever before. There also is visible a relatively new phenomenon of routing around it, marking a world without the West with its own distinctive set of rules, institutions, and relationships. It cannot be taken as a given that the optimal model for a just society is the American one. Among the many global public opinion polls that have upset Americans in the last decade, perhaps the one that should have been most disturbing asked this question: "Suppose a young person who wanted to leave this country asked you to recommend where to go to lead a good life; what country would you recommend?" In only one country was the United States the first choice.[6] No single alternative model is on the verge of replacing an old one, but TINA is giving way to THEMBA—"there must be an alternative."

It's a marketplace not a war of ideas. Outside of the physical battlefields of interstate conflict, Americans in the second half of the twentieth century fought a war on poverty, a war on drugs, a war on cancer, and at least a few others. In late 2001 the federal government launched a self-proclaimed war of ideas against violent radical terrorist movements. The war metaphor is crisp, actionable, and morally compelling: what American doesn't want to win a war against fanaticism, hate, and intolerance? But it dangerously distorts the policy challenge. The global competition of ideas is not a war. It is not the domain of armies and generals. There are no shock-and-awe tactics, no decisive victories, no unconditional surrenders. You cannot achieve a final victory in a war of ideas, because it is not a war at all but a competition within a marketplace. The rules of engagement are much closer to those set out by social and economic thinkers such as John Stuart Mill and Milton Friedman than those set out by the Prussian military strategist Carl von Clausewitz. This marketplace is built around an evolving digital infrastructure that increasingly connects everyone to everyone. To win is to gain market share among consumers; global publics pick and choose what most attracts them. A marketplace, unlike a battlefield, contains many competitors—a fully global competition of ideas.

There was a strong sense in 2008 and 2009, at least among a certain political swathe of the American electorate and elite, that global systems would swing back to "normal" (with America at the center of the international political universe) after the presidency of George W. Bush. If Bush was the problem, then the election of 2008 was the solution. The United States would reset its foreign policy to a modified version of what worked in the Cold War against communism. We would reinvoke America's historical legacy: the Founders' vision of a "city on a Hille"; Lincoln's "last best hope of mankind"; Wilson's belief that the United States would "make the world safe for democracy." While getting our groove back, we would tweak our public diplomacy to better disseminate America's message.

It hasn't worked out that way, which should come as no great surprise. There's nothing wrong with a serious and thoughtful look backward toward historical legacies. It's essential. Any plausible foreign policy strategy will tap traditional American values. But a competitive leadership proposition for today and tomorrow's world fundamentally has to be *adaptive* not *restorative*, forward- not backward-looking, and capable of addressing those reopened big questions in ways that fit the present century, not the last one.

At the core of such an effort are new, more modern conceptions of world order and a just society that are embedded in a vision of the future which inspires and embraces global populations. We develop these ideas in Chapters 3 and 4. We begin this process in Chapter 2 by explaining more deeply the guiding logic of a global competition of ideas and the dynamics of that marketplace.

Chapter 5 builds on the notion of a revised vision of the future and puts the leadership proposition into practice by posing and framing four hard choices that together add up to an American strategy.

No single book can address all the important aspects of American foreign policy. This is a book that emphasizes how beliefs, ideologies, and ideas matter in the theory and practice of U.S. foreign policy. Our purpose is not to judge the big ideas of politics and society such as truth and justice, or to offer revolutionary new ones. Our objectives are fundamentally pragmatic and prescriptive, and so in this book we leave aside abstract political theory and philosophy. We want to explain how ideologies work in contemporary international politics and why foreign policy makers should pay very close attention. We want to put forward an argument about competition among ideologies that explains how that competition has become central to power and influence in world politics. And we want to suggest practical mindsets, strategies, and even some tactics for American foreign policy makers to multiply and maximize, for the good, America's capability and impact in that world.

Our message, though deeply challenging, is a profoundly optimistic one. To take our arguments seriously would mean to reconfigure how American policy makers think about and act upon core concepts like liberalism, soft power, democracy, and openness in the twenty-first century. The good news is that there really is no society or country on the planet better situated to playing and prevailing in this global competition of ideas. But policy makers must see the game clearly for what it really is, and play it much more proficiently than they have thus far.

Some may try to pin on us the label of "declinists" when it comes to the United States or "apologists" when it comes to others. On the contrary, we push back against the culture of denial that really puts America's global position at risk. Competing in this new age of ideology is among the most important strategic tasks for American foreign policy makers. Ideological competition is fundamentally a matter of power, which should make this book's message amenable to foreign policy thinkers regardless of how they situate themselves on the political spectrum. We are not talking about power for the sake of power, but power for the sake of influence in world politics, which depends on national power, broadly conceived. It was Hans Morgenthau, the grand old man of modern American realism, who warned against the power-sapping effects of "residues of formerly adequate modes of thought and action now rendered obsolete by a new social reality."[7] It is not naive to pay attention to the importance of ideas, and it is utter blindness to ignore them altogether.

The U.S. role in the new world order should not be a strictly defensive one. Some governments and some ideologies will try to erect new barriers to entry as a way of protecting what they have to offer in this ideological competition. The United States could not do so and remain true to what is distinctively American. Instead, the United States could implement a new leadership strategy for a more global system rather than continuing

in the vein of older challenges of containing communism or defeating terrorism. A lot of other international
players—other countries, global corporations, megaphilanthropies, religious movements, Internet communities—will try hard to beat the United States to it. And so
the new age of ideology is going to be very interesting and
very competitive.

We have no easy solutions to offer, nor reassurance that
the United States can "have its cake and eat it too" in international politics. Competition and strategy, as ever,
are about making thoughtful choices and assessing in
a straightforward manner what can be achieved, what
will work, and which risks are worth taking. The United
States must base its future strategy on an assumption as
basic and world-changing as that of Copernicus; it must
"face the facts, as they say, with both eyes open." There really is no better place to start.

2

A GLOBAL COMPETITION OF IDEAS

In autumn 2003 Donald Rumsfeld asked his top advisors this now famous question: "Are we capturing, killing or deterring and dissuading more terrorists every day than the madrassas and the radical clerics are recruiting, training and deploying against us?"

This was, and remains, a reasonable question. What is America's strategy for getting to a reasonable answer? The way the former secretary of defense phrased the choice offered four options for protecting America's interests: To capture, kill, deter, or dissuade those who pose threats to the United States. With some shifts in emphasis and formulation, the Obama administration has been pursuing the same options. In rough terms, the first two are functions of "hard power"—the use of military force, carried out with boots on the ground as well as drones in the air. The goal is to be systematic; the risk is to end up in a game of Whac-a-Mole™. Either way, at least to an extent, there is the advantage of being self-actualizing: you don't have to convince the dead terrorist that he is dead in order to achieve the goal.

The second two are a kind of "soft power."[1] That is because deterrence and dissuasion are not statements about physical reality or the world outside the terrorist's mind. They are outcomes within that mind, a function of ideas. Deterrence works when a person believes that the costs of taking an action exceed the expected benefits. Dissuasion means that the potential terrorist sees compelling reasons not to do what he or she is otherwise tempted to do.

We can change the world around the terrorist all we want, but (unless we kill or capture all of them) it is ultimately the calculation within a person's mind that matters for his or her behavior—and that we are trying to affect. Put simply, the target of our foreign policy is the ideas in other peoples' heads. That is why a phrase like "winning hearts and minds," as easy as it can be to ridicule, is at the end of the day a deathly serious matter for U.S. foreign policy. Even at this very basic level, it's a contest between the ideas we want them to believe and some other ideas that we really don't want them to believe.

Ideas Do Not Fight Wars; They Compete

It's no wonder we hear so much about the "war" of ideas. It is a heavily used paradigm, as any Internet search will reveal. "We will also wage a war of ideas," the Bush administration declared in its *National Security Strategy of the United States*. "Engage the struggle of ideas," urged the 9-11

Commission. A host of books and policy papers from liberal progressive think tanks and scholars have issued their own clarion calls to the ideological battlefront. Although the Obama administration has tried to drop the "war" metaphor, the prevalent narrative and much of the political debate still are cast in these terms.[2]

But the "war on terrorism" metaphor undermines its own mission. It's misguided in its focus. The issues raised by the reopening of those five big questions stressed in Chapter 1 are about much more than freedom versus fundamentalism. It is also misguided in its scope. The new age of ideology is global, not just a battle between the West and Islam. And finally, it is misguided in its dynamics. Ideas don't fight wars against each other, they compete. So whereas the emphasis on ideas is valid and appropriate, the war metaphor is not. The United States is facing not a global war of ideas but a global marketplace of ideas. And the marketplace requires a very different analytic framework, which will in turn drive a different and more effective set of policies.

These are not just semantic fine points. Metaphors matter. Policy discussions and choices unfold differently under different structuring metaphors. We should have learned by now from the failures of other war metaphors—the war on poverty, the war on drugs, the war on cancer—that rhetorical flourish is one thing, effective policy quite another. The stakes of one metaphor are no lower or higher than the stakes of the other. It is instead a strategy choice, and there's little chance of getting a strategy right if you get the setting wrong.

Consider the schema that may go through the head of a policy maker when the notion of war is invoked. Wars have generals who make strategic decisions and soldiers who follow orders along a hierarchy of command and control. Whether the doctrine has been World War II–style unconditional surrender; or post-Vietnam Powell Doctrine, using force decisively in the service of clearly defined goals; or Iraq-induced counterinsurgency; or some other military doctrine, the goal of war is victory: to defeat the enemy, dismantle its resources of power, and change its organizing principles.[3]

The metaphor continues. If this is a war of ideas, surely we would need a strong deterrent—the concept being that if we have in place a credible threat to crush a hurtful idea that might arise, then, knowing that, a potential adversary would never actually put the idea into play. We would need robust defenses and a multilayered immune system that can prevent hostile ideas from entering our borders, destroying them if they somehow get in. We might even think about pre-emptive attacks on troubling ideas that threaten us by trying to prevent their development. If only we could simply understand where the relevant ideas came from and how they will evolve!

Does any of this make sense when it comes to the realm of ideas? Of course it doesn't. Particularly not for a society like ours, that draws its inspiration and continuing energy from democratic discourse and debate. One of America's great political, cultural, and economic strengths has been our willingness to argue among ourselves and be proven wrong—without resorting to war.

Today's government policy can be reversed tomorrow if a new president or coalition successfully convinces the necessary players that it's time to change. Our cultural life is filled with artists who pose the previously unthinkable, who seek to challenge the most cherished beliefs and commitments, all so that we don't become overconfident about things we think we know for certain. We don't fight wars against artists we disagree with, we critique them. And our economic success is built on the relentlessness of market discipline, which values ideas that work over those that don't and transfers assets from the latter to the former—without violence.

Venture capitalists live in the world of the pitch—convince me that your idea is a good one and you can have 10 million dollars to make it happen. Hold a gun to my head, and you'll get nothing. There's no place for a war of ideas inside the United States, which is why terms like "the culture wars" deserve a negative connotation in American public discourse. When someone tells you they feel like they are in the middle of the culture wars, that's a signal of failure, not success.

It should be no different when we look outside America's borders. In today's connected world, where information, images, and reports of action travel at the speed of light to every corner of the earth, it is no longer possible for a presumptive world leader to propose the legitimacy of one principle of political and social organization for his or her own country, another for everyone else's, and a third for the international environment.

When it comes to a leadership proposition, the competition among ideas is now all one game. Even if the specifics of the rules can differ reasonably in implementation from place to place, they can't stand at odds with each other. Any hypocrisy will immediately rise to the surface, and its painful visibility will undermine a leadership proposition in short order.

In other words, when Americans say that U.S. citizens have the right or even the obligation to listen to others and can generally manage civil discourse, without violence, and work their way through debate and discussion to an outcome best for a complex society, then we will have to take quite seriously the notion that those living elsewhere can do exactly the same, though they may come to different conclusions. And this implies that all global citizens can do so together.

The downside of pretending otherwise is not just the potential to be hated or resented for hypocrisy—although that is in itself a meaningfully bad thing for U.S. foreign policy. There is a downside much more immediate and tangible. We suspect that promoting the notion of a war of ideas is self-defeating for the United States, and not just when it comes to the leadership proposition we want to offer to the rest of the world. There is significant risk to core American interests if the struggle against terrorism or violent extremism continues to be, and be seen as, a profound war of ideologies.

The reason is simple. It is impossible to imagine a world in which some ideology somewhere will not produce a few thousand people who believe it is their destiny or calling to destroy the United States. We cannot rely for security on the imaginary goal of cleansing the world entirely and forever of such ideologies, because it is not possible to do that.

And so a war of ideologies easily becomes an endless war. That is a place where escalation does not play to U.S. strengths but rather to the strengths of violent extremists. The Cold War was entirely different. The Soviets and the Americans had a profoundly shared risk of escalation—if nuclear weapons came into play, neither side would benefit from escalation. Both sides knew that. So a self-limiting dynamic emerged. In the contemporary context ideological escalation will tend to benefit groups like al-Qaeda more than it does the United States, simply because al-Qaeda has less to lose. Indeed, escalation is precisely al-Qaeda's goal. Policy makers in Washington have fallen into that trap before.

Ideologies contend for the commitment of individual human beings. They always have, and they always will. And they are always in competition with each other: incessant, relentless, sometimes brutal competition. But it is fundamentally a global competition of ideas, not a war. If we take that new metaphor seriously, remaking our policies in line with its logic, the United States will find itself over time in what we now think of as a "winning" position. So, what if we start from the notion that ideas meet each other not on a battlefield but in something much more like a marketplace? What if we decide the rules of engagement are closer to those set out by John Stuart Mill for conducting a search for truth than those set out for "war as politics by other means" in the writings of von Clausewitz?

We would then be driven to fashion a new form of leadership, one much better suited to the world of the present and the future than nostalgic visions of our post–World War II leadership role. This means leadership for a Copernican world order, one in which the United States does not start from the presumption that it is at the center of everyone else's view of the universe.

In a functioning modern marketplace of ideas, at least three things are true of a twenty-first-century leadership proposition. First, we offer, but they choose. A market leader is fundamentally more dependent on the followers than the followers are on the leader. That is because presumptive leaders make offers, not diktats, and presumptive followers make choices. Eventually they choose those offers they find most attractive. Followers may sign up and close off other options for a while, but not for a long while.

Second, the relationships are visible and consistency is demanded. Market leaders don't depend heavily on private deals and subterfuge to hold their bargains in place. A high level of transparency prevails: as on a modern stock market, everyone has access to a great deal of the information about what they are choosing to buy (or not buy). Presumptive leaders who say different and inconsistent things about what they offer to different possible constituencies find themselves in trouble very quickly.

Finally, there is real competition. Markets are relentless in their ability to generate new offerings. In the face of that fact, powerful leaders often believe, and will try to convince wavering followers, that the alternative to existing leadership is chaos.[4] That's the TINA story, and it's rarely true. More important, the players in the market rarely believe it for long. Even if they stay in the leader's camp, competition serves their interests well by forcing the leader to continually improve what he or she is offering.

Competitiveness: A Necessary Obsession

International relations scholars sometimes say that the United States has never really been a normal state. What that means is that for much of its early history, the United States relied on its geography, two oceans, and immense domestic resources and riches to stay out of much standard geopolitical maneuvering. While the European great powers of the 1800s practiced statecraft in constant competition with each other for economic and military power and control, the United States used the luxury of geographic separation to pick and choose, selectively, which European issues it would engage. Within the Western hemisphere, the Monroe Doctrine early on established the United States as a country determined to be, and quite soon capable of being, a unilateral rule maker, or de facto hegemon. After an important but unsustained intervention in the intricate European politics of World War I, the United States went back, so far as it could, to a splendid isolationism. The Smoot-Hawley Tariff Act, at least partly responsible for setting off a worldwide retaliatory trade closure that contributed to the global Great Depression, was in some sense the ultimate manifestation of an economic nationalist mindset. The mid-1930s

Ludlow constitutional amendment, which would have required a national referendum before any decision to go to war, came within a few votes of passing in Congress. Despite President Franklin D. Roosevelt's proddings, America did what Congress thought was good for America in the troubled days of the 1930s; what it meant for the rest of the world was, well, not really our concern.

World War II pierced that bubble of splendid isolationism. For the second time in a half-century the United States found itself deeply engaged in a massive and nearly global conflict. Even then, however, Arthur Schlesinger, Jr. quotes FDR as worrying that "anybody who thinks isolationism is dead in this country is crazy. As soon as this war is over, it may well be stronger than ever."[5] Indeed, once victory was achieved there was a rapid demobilization, another yearning to "bring the boys home" and get back to normal—only to be confronted by the Soviet threat and the Cold War. With intellectual prodding from people like George Kennan and Hans Morgenthau, and organizations like the Council on Foreign Relations, isolationist impulses were contained. The Korean War in some sense cemented the consensus: the debate was no longer about whether the United States should engage globally, it was about the terms and extent of that engagement. Some foreign observers, particularly in Great Britain, saw U.S. emergence as a long-awaited maturation in the field of great power politics.

It was a historically peculiar maturation, however, that skipped an important step. In its global footprint the United States leaped from insulation to hegemony. In the 1920s the U.S. government wanted nothing more than to be left out of international political games. In the late 1940s, possessing the world's most powerful and technologically advanced military, and with roughly half of global gross domestic product (GDP), the United States was in a position to dictate most of the rules for the post–World War II game, almost never needing to engage the subtle intricacies, the give and take of great power politics. Indeed for almost half a century it never had to play the diplomatic game as other great powers did.

Much of that is good news, as any historian of nineteenth-century European diplomacy will tell you. But here's the bad news: The United States almost never had to take account of others' desires and goals as much as those countries had to take account of ours. In short, the United States never really competed on an even playing field.

Hegemony leads to arrogance, and that breeds annoyance and resentment among those who have to deal with the hegemon, even a relatively benign one. There was no shortage of either in the post–World War II world. But there was also no shortage of far-sighted, inspired strategic thinking and behavior by U.S. foreign policy makers. John Ruggie, John Ikenberry, and Anne-Marie Slaughter, among others, make an important point about this period: the inevitable errors notwithstanding, the United States played an extraordinary role, setting up significant pillars of a liberal world order that was a great success not only for America but also for many other parts of the world.[6] As hegemonies go, this was a fairly enlightened one.

The U.S.-inspired order helped to transform much of

Europe into a peaceful and prosperous continent. It facilitated decolonization, even if it failed to manage some of the consequences well. It gave birth to a surprisingly robust financial system and a relatively free trade system, and these would support with reasonable consistency a period of unprecedented economic expansion and later globalization. Measured against other historical examples, against the system that the Russians set up on their side of the Iron Curtain, and against counterfactual histories of what might have been had the hegemon been a state other than America, this was an extraordinarily successful period for U.S. foreign policy. Yet what many would see as a benign hegemony was still a hegemony.

The first twenty years of the Cold War taught us bilateral nuclear statecraft and its critical sub-discipline, superpower crisis management. The big foreign-policy problem of this era was containment, and that rested on managing a military balance of terror in the face of rolling crises over points of contention like Berlin, with nuclear weapons always lurking in the background. The central insight of Thomas Schelling in his classic work *The Strategy of Conflict* was that the contest between the United States and the Soviet Union was fundamentally a game of intertwined psychologies, with each using threats, promises, and other signals to try to change the beliefs that one side held about the other's intentions and commitments.[7] But this too was less a normal competition than it was a behavioral manifestation of game theory—a repeated game of "chicken" or "prisoner's dilemma" played out on a global stage.

During the 1970s and 1980s America learned about modern economic competition for the first time on a global scale. With the collapse of the Bretton Woods peg, two oil shocks, the onset of stagflation, and the ensuing economic malaise of the 1970s, the United States found itself facing real competitors for leadership in late industrial mass production and technology. In 1980, the World Economic Forum began publishing its annual "World Competitiveness Report" to judge and rank the economic performance of nations. In 1981 Ronald Reagan took office with Americans seriously wondering if the Germans and the Japanese had figured out a better way to do capitalism. This was a significant intellectual discontinuity for the American decision-making elite. What exactly did it mean to compete with a country such as Japan that seemed to play the economic game by a different set of rules?

It is notable, in retrospect, that it took nearly a decade for the United States to sort out what it believed and what should be done. It was a long, hard, and occasionally bizarre adaptation. The list of dysfunctional, self-inflicted wounds that the U.S. government brought upon itself during this period is legendary. It tried to stem the flow of high quality, fuel-efficient Japanese cars into the U.S. market by establishing Voluntary Export Restrictions (VERs), a soft form of import quota. The Japanese automakers took their resulting profits and responded by building factories and manufacturing their cars inside the United States. Congress pressed the Japanese to open their domestic market to U.S. exports—to little avail in most cases. There was talk of trade wars, veiled threats about the sustainability of the U.S.-Japanese alliance in the face of trade deficits, near-panic over purchases (at inflated prices!) by Japanese investors of iconic properties like Pebble Beach and Rockefeller Center.

There was also a small avalanche of books and articles demanding that the Japanese change their business practices, laws, and even their society and culture so that the competition would be more "fair." Between 1989 and 1993, the two countries engaged in talks under a process called the "Structural Impediments Initiative," which was supposed to reach down deeply into both sides' domestic political economy in order to modify practices that stood in the way of fair trade and competition. Who knows how much more difficult and tense the situation might have become had the Japanese economy not fallen into a decade-long recession during the 1990s?

What's just as notable about this story is the intellectual ferment it caused around the concept of competitiveness. You might think it was a simple notion, but American economists, pundits, and policy makers treated it as if it were anything but. Ira Magaziner and Robert Reich argued that competitiveness in high-value-added industries was essential to America's standard of living—and at serious risk. Lester Thurow warned us that nations must compete in world markets just as corporations do, and that any nation failing to match others in productivity or technology would face a crisis much like companies face when they can't match the costs and products of rival firms. In 1986, a high-profile group of industrial, university, and labor leaders founded in Washington, D.C. the Council on Competitiveness, whose self-proclaimed mission was to "elevate national competitiveness to the forefront of national consciousness."

In sum, a competitive mindset toward other nations did not even emerge in the United States until the 1980s, and it took a decade to sink in. Eventually it did become necessary background knowledge for thinking about America's role in the economic world, at least. When Paul Krugman in 1994 wrote his cogent *Foreign Affairs* critique of the concept of competitiveness, which he called a "dangerous obsession," it was the critique that proved the point.[8] Krugman took to task policy makers who used the rhetoric of competitiveness to justify self-serving policies. He questioned some elements of the analogy between countries in the global economy and firms in markets. He highlighted how sloppy (and just plain fictitious) economic reasoning about issues like the trade deficit and productivity had worked their way into the political debate. And, most important, he explained why national economic competitiveness should not be thought of as a zero-sum game, in which a win for the United States had to be a loss for Japan or anyone else. But he never said that America didn't have to compete in the global economy, because that was now a background assumption. The point of Krugman's intervention was to help Americans understand more precisely the nature of that competition.

The collapse of the Japanese economy in the 1990s may have taken away the immediate stimulus, but it didn't touch the deeper shift in American mindsets. Competitiveness was a constant trope in the Clinton administration's economic message and policies. And it was just as central a message in the 2000s under the Bush administration. No serious economic policy proposal could today be put on the table in Washington without an accompanying claim about how it enhances our ability to compete in world markets.

Yet the mindset was still strikingly different in the 1990s when it came to geopolitics. Would the United States really have to compete with others in a serious way on this playing field? One can see why geopolitics seemed to be not much of a competition. Not only the Cold War ended in 1989; it was also the de facto end of the opposing superpower. The Iraq War of 1990–91 was not just a win, it was an unprecedented demonstration of America's overwhelming capacity—the ability to project power halfway around the world and defeat a massive land army with unbelievably few American casualties.

The euphoria was so great that President George H. W. Bush heralded "a new world order where diverse nations are drawn together in common cause to achieve the universal aspirations of mankind: peace and security, freedom and the rule of law."[9] The harder edge to this thinking came through in the Defense Policy Guidance (DPG) developed by Dick Cheney, then secretary of defense, which cast the principal objective of U.S. foreign policy as one of "prevent[ing] the re-emergence of a new rival," indeed preventing "potential competitors from even aspiring to a larger regional or global role."[10] Although the

Bush White House rushed to disown the DPG once it leaked, it still stood along with NSC-68, the blueprint developed by the Truman presidency for winning the Cold War, as one of the most influential documents never officially adopted—especially when Cheney and co-authors Paul Wolfowitz, Lewis "Scooter" Libby, and others came back into power in the George W. Bush administration. In the interim this triumphalism was captured in Charles Krauthammer's classic phrase, the "unipolar moment."[11]

Even though the Clinton administration toned down the rhetoric, it also held to a view of extraordinary U.S. preponderance. This was the essence of America as "the indispensable nation" (a phrase usually attributed to Secretary of State Madeleine Albright but first put forward by journalist James Chace).[12] It was always overstated: much was happening in the world despite and without the United States. India and Pakistan tested nuclear weapons despite U.S. opposition. Arabs and Israelis did not get to yes despite U.S. peace brokering. The International Criminal Court was created without U.S. participation. So too the Kyoto Protocol. So too the Ottawa Treaty to ban land mines.

The George W. Bush administration saw these events as exceptions to the rule, a consequence of Clinton-Gore softness more than systemic dynamics. "Power matters," the Bush team proclaimed back in the 2000 presidential campaign. Unlike the Democrats, too many of whom "are (and always have been) uncomfortable with the notions of power," the president and his "Vulcans" would assert American power, not apologize for it.[13] They would focus

on the U.S. national interest, not cloud strategic thinking with naive idealist notions and mushy multilatera-
list pseudo-aspirations. Even before the second Iraq War,
the Bush administration had established an in-your-face
approach to global diplomacy—pronouncing the Kyoto
treaty "dead on arrival," writing off international law as
"deeply and perhaps irrevocably flawed," and repeatedly
castigating the United Nations.[14] "Has George Bush ever
met a treaty that he liked?" the *Economist* editorialized. "It
is hard to avoid the suspicion that it is the very idea of
multilateral cooperation that Mr. Bush objects to."[15]

And then came Iraq, which was of course never really
just about Iraq. The removal of Saddam Hussein was to
be a definitive demonstration of overwhelming American
power, the birthing of Iraqi democracy a manifestation
of that power married to American principles. The message would go out throughout the Middle East that the
United States was intent on remaking the region as less
roguish and more democratic. And globally whatever
doubts may still have been out there, whether about
American will or capacity, would be dispelled. The United
States would lead, and others needed to follow or get out
of the way.

The Vulcans were right about one thing: Iraq has had
a demonstration effect, though largely the opposite of
what was intended. And the unipolar moment became
just that—a moment, not the enduring and encompass-
ing new system that neoconservatives envisioned. The Pew
polls documented America's low standing in these years.
An American Political Science Association task force

made a compelling case that this was not just an atmospheric but mattered in practical and substantive ways for foreign policy capacity.[16]

Much of the argumentation and rhetoric about unipolarity and the like rested on a fundamental overestimation of U.S. power. To be more precise, it rested on a fundamental *underestimation* of both the creative and destructive potential of other human beings and countries. In the Copernican reality, these independently minded individuals, groups, and nations, in pursuit of their own goals, have incentives to "design around" U.S. strategies so that that they don't have to confront them head on. And human beings are remarkably innovative when it comes to doing that.

Perhaps if U.S. foreign policy makers had been thinking more clearly about the competitive environment of world politics and the creative options others can invent as they develop their strategies for competing, it would have been easier to see the destructive potential of al-Qaeda in the summer of 2001. Or to see the emerging insurgency in Iraq for what it was a year or more before it did. Or to understand more deeply the insecurities and vulnerabilities, as well as the ambitions, that rest in the minds of decision makers in Beijing, Moscow, Delhi, Brasilia, Tehran, Doha, and elsewhere.

The reality of geopolitics is that everybody competes— and Schelling's core arguments about game theory are always in play. Although the United States may sometimes be powerful enough to pick the geopolitical game that others need to play, it can almost never by itself determine the outcome, because others get to pick their own strategies against ours. Again, this is as obvious and intuitive a point as seeking competitiveness in the global economy, yet it is one that remains difficult for America to really accept.

How much harder still for the United States to think about competing in the realm of ideology! Consider some excerpts from the Bush administration's National Security Strategy Document of 2002. This is the first sentence of the Introduction, which came under the direct signature of the president:

> The great struggles of the twentieth century between liberty and totalitarianism ended with a decisive victory for the forces of freedom—and a single sustainable model for national success: freedom, democracy, and free enterprise.

And then:

> People everywhere want to be able to speak freely; choose who will govern them; worship as they please; educate their children—male and female; own property; and enjoy the benefits of their labor. These values of freedom are right and true for every person, in every society—and the duty of protecting these values against their enemies is the common calling of freedom-loving people across the globe and across the ages.[17]

These are powerful sentiments, powerfully expressed. The problem is, it is mostly wishful thinking. Ideological disagreements have never ended in a decisive victory that closes down alternatives. They probably never will, as long as human minds are part of the equation. The notion of a single sustainable model for national success simply does not resonate with the majority of people on this planet. Ask, for example, the 300 million Chinese citizens that have been lifted out of poverty in the last twenty years. Or the hundreds of millions whose boats have not been lifted by globalization's rising tide and for whom democracy has not delivered much. The notion that "people everywhere" want the same thing is belied by casual observation of what they do and say about what they want. And to claim that values we hold dear—freedom in particular as we define it—are "right and true for every person, in every society" ignores and disrespects other historical and cultural traditions.

The 2008 election of Barack Hussein Obama, biracial and with family ties spanning three continents, helped both in the diversity inherent to his persona and the policy shifts promised. But two other dynamics have become apparent. One is that while negative reputation created disincentives for cooperating with the United States, positive reputation did not foster comparable incentives. In the runup to the Iraq War both the Turkish and Indian defense ministers indicated willingness to cooperate with the United States, but had to back off in the face of anti-Bush legislative and political opposition at home. But pro-Obama sentiment has not been enough to garner international cooperation on U.S. priority issues. European North Atlantic Treaty Organization (NATO) allies have not significantly ramped up their commitments to Afghanistan; indeed in early 2010 the issue brought down the Dutch government. UN sanctions against Iran were tough sledding. Saudi Arabia remained reluctant to activate its Arab Peace Initiative even when urged by President Obama on the eve of his major "new beginning" speech to the Arab world. A negative reputation depletes a nation's power, but a positive reputation does not seem to comparably enhance it.

Second is the Obama administration's own tension within its world view. Its 2010 National Security Strategy (NSS) recognizes on its very first page that "no one nation—no matter how powerful—can meet global challenges alone."[18] It thus speaks less of unilaterally wielding power than "galvanizing the collective action that can serve common interests." Indeed it uses the terms *common* or *shared interests* ten times, and *mutual* almost thirty times. Ultimately, though, it is about "renewing American leadership so that we can more effectively advance *our* interests in the 21st century" (italics added). To be sure, any national security strategy in a nation-state world has to have its own national interest at its core. But others don't make the claim to leadership that the United States does (the word *leader* mentioned sixty times in this document). What about when advancing American interests is not the same as serving common interests? Indeed, are interests as mutual as posited? If not, then it is less a collective action problem than a competitive environment. Moreover, is the American way always the optimal one for achieving mutuality? Although the Obama approach is much less dismissive of such questions than the Bush one was, it has its own unresolved orientations.

Don't misunderstand our argument. We believe deeply and profoundly in democracy, freedom, market economics, human dignity, and tolerance of religious and other differences. We believe that America has built extraordinary institutions to put these values into practice. But even before getting to claims of their generalizability and universality, there is plenty of basis for questioning whether they are working as well as our invocations claim. Some still take heed of Churchill's oft-cited comment that "Americans will always do the right thing, after they've exhausted all the alternatives." Perhaps. But it will only be so through creativity, not complacency.

It may be that American ideas are the best ideas about humanity and society that will ever be invented. It may be that one day in the future everyone will believe in them and act accordingly. We actually doubt that, because no idea is perfect for everyone and for all time, and because human beings will always be searching for better ideas. But it really doesn't matter. For a serious discussion about making better foreign policy in a time frame that is relevant to decision makers, these debates don't need to be settled theologically. They can be set aside for political philosophers. Instead, U.S. policy makers should get serious about how to compete most effectively in the vibrant, bubbling, energetic, creative, occasionally infuriating marketplace of ideas that is global politics. You can't win the war because war is not the game. What you can do is compete, every day, against every alternative and rival that is competing with us.

Public diplomacy addresses part of this. Initially after 9-11 public diplomacy was largely premised on the belief that "they" wouldn't hate "us" if the diplomatic message was communicated effectively. The message was assumed to be accurate, just in need of better marketing. But this was the approach of vendor selling, not the approach of consumer choice. Some think-tank studies have improved upon this.[19] University programs such as the University of Southern California's Center on Public Diplomacy are professionalizing the career track. Groups such as Business for Diplomatic Action have engaged elements of the private sector that see the link between "brand America" and bottom lines. Public diplomacy (PD) even has its own under-secretary in the State Department.

Yet while such efforts can help at the margins, they do not sufficiently muster up to how much ideas matter, and what it will take for the United States to compete in this twenty-first-century global marketplace of ideas. American foreign policy experts need to become at least as serious about ideological competition, and as proficient, as American capitalists have become about economic competition.

An Evolving Global Marketplace of Ideas

To this point, we have addressed the reality and necessity of the global competition of ideas, but we have really only hinted about the shape of the playing field on which that competition now takes place. It is not the same playing field as it was sixty or for that matter even ten years ago. Here's a story (a true one) that says a lot about what the contemporary playing field actually looks like.

In the spring of 2007, the Russian Federal Customs Service suddenly and without warning shut down the export from Russia of all human medical biological materials, including blood and human tissue. In the several years prior, Russia had become a destination of choice for large pharmaceutical firms, many of them based in the United States, to carry out clinical trials for new drugs. Such trials are increasingly sent off-shore to developing countries, where the costs of recruiting and retaining patients can be as little as one-tenth what it costs inside the United States. Russia is a particularly attractive location for offshore clinical trials because the Russian hospital system treats all patients who have similar symptoms on the same hospital ward. Trials by U.S.-based firms had tripled between 2003 and 2006 and were set to increase further. The ban on export of biological material essentially closed down this enterprise, because specimens could not be analyzed by labs with the necessary equipment and expertise, most of which are outside Russia.

Why would the Russian government walk away from what seemed to be a mutually profitable arrangement? After all, the pharmaceutical companies were getting cheap and convenient access to a good clinical trial population; Russian patients enrolled in trials were receiving new drugs and a standard of care that they otherwise could not have had. This was not, as some might think, an ethical backlash against using Russians as "guinea pigs" for Western medications or a real-life pharmacological scandal like that portrayed in John Le Carré's fictional novel *The Constant Gardener.* Here is what happened. The move, according to the Russian newspaper *Kommersant*, followed on a report given to President Vladimir Putin by the Russian Federal Security Service, which claimed that Western pharmaceutical companies might be using the Russian biological materials to develop genetically engineered ethnically specific biological weapons.

Paranoia? Conspiracy theory? Bargaining tactic? Unfounded fear? Economic protectionism cloaked in science fiction scenarios? It may be a bit of all of those things. It barely matters. The issue is not whether these allegations have even the slightest grain of truth.

The issue is what this story suggests about the competitive landscape of ideas in today's world—where ideas come from, how they operate, and how ideas contend with each other for claims on human action. The rational actor models that are today popular in academic political science simply beg the most important question: How do the actors (rational or otherwise) on the other side of the marketplace of ideas evaluate the claims that are being made about what is true, what is good, what is a benefit, and what is a cost?

There is no single general answer to that question in international politics, any more than there would be if we were talking about a marketplace for cars, television shows, or fashion. There are some general characteristics of the marketplace of ideas that we can specify for the present and the next decade. The topography that we see has four main characteristics.

An evolving global digital infrastructure. There is an evolving global digital infrastructure that will increasingly connect everyone to everyone, but not on equal terms nor at equal density. Hype aside, the world really is in the midst of a communications revolution spawned by Internet technology. It is changing many things about the ways ideas compete by changing how people talk to and argue with each other about what they are experiencing and what they do (or should) believe. If you can get past the hype, you will find profound and relevant messages embedded in some of what is being said about the Internet.

The most obvious, but also the most important change, is simply that governments and other official sources of information are no longer the key brokers of credibility (if they ever really were). Absent government censorship, just about everyone on the planet has, or will soon have, easy access to a cacophony of voices, a multiplicity of narratives, all starting from a more or less equal place when it comes to their ability to reach an audience. The Internet and its associated technologies are a "force multiplier" for many forms of persuasion and storytelling, and thus for part of what goes under the label of soft power. The Internet boosts soft power projection capability radically, while distributing those capabilities more widely and broadly. Governments are just one voice among many, and in some ways the least magnetic to many people simply because they are the least novel.

It's not just voices that are now engaged. More precisely, it is not just words. What was invented a few decades ago as a technological medium for the transmission of computer code and simple text became in the late 1990s and early 2000s a worldwide medium for the transmission of linked multimedia documents through protocols that we call the World Wide Web. Now, we are in the full throes of transition to a worldwide medium of visual images—pictures, movies, and soon enough three-dimensional renderings.

Call it the YouTube phenomenon if you like. And although it is sometimes easy to dismiss things like YouTube as a passing fad of amateur producers and voyeurs, it is in fact the quite profound early signal of an utterly serious means of communication in the global competition of ideas. Human beings are visual animals and they respond strongly to images and pictures, often more strongly than to arguments rendered in black text on a white page. Al-Qaeda recruiting videos are quite different from Sayid Qtub's books or the Unabomber's manifesto. Cell-phone pictures and camcorder movies of protesters in Ukraine or monks being shot by Myanmar security forces carry the sort of immediate and poignant emotional impact that a newspaper article generally cannot. Among the populations from which violent extremists are most likely to be recruited just now, does anyone remember the legal niceties in John Yoo's memoranda about what does and does not constitute torture? Does anyone *not* remember the image of the hooded Abu Ghraib prisoner standing on a box with wires connected to his arms?

When it comes to arguments between and among contending ideas, the terms of debate used with images versus texts are very different. Put differently, the rules and processes of rational deliberation that Westerners tend to associate with Enlightenment thinking are mostly about how words argue with words. What do we really know about how pictures argue with pictures? How does one argue with or change the mind of someone who believes in the meaning behind the Abu Ghraib photos? There are probably workable answers to that question, but we are only at the beginning of understanding them. They certainly have not been articulated in a meaningful way for foreign policy makers operating in the global competition of ideas.

The global digital infrastructure that will make these arguments possible is breaking down many traditional boundaries—between people, religions, economies, and societies. One of the hardest and most important questions that such boundary dissolution raises is whether or not this is a good thing for the United States. It should be, in one sense. It is almost an article of faith (although often held implicitly) that the United States benefits disproportionately from boundary-dissolving technological change. The reason why is simple: Americans believe they are a state and society uniquely well positioned to evolve through the kind of change that shakes up old categories and makes people rethink their affiliations.

Although we want this proposition to be true, we believe that it needs much greater scrutiny—and a consequent change in our actions—to make it operational. That is because it is too simple to assume that a shared global digital infrastructure necessarily empowers a broad and open marketplace of goods and ideas. It can do that, but by nature it needn't.

Consider a function on the Amazon.com Web site: "people who bought this book also bought . . ." The technical term for this function is *affiliative sorting*—the ability to scan a massive forest efficiently to find the trees that are similar on some important dimension (in the realm of ideas, the people or ideas with which you affiliate). Affiliative sorting is the holy grail of commerce. It allows marketers to approach self-segmented populations who choose their own defining criteria.

But what is very good for commerce can be very bad for politics. When affiliative sorting connects like with like in the realm of ideas, it almost has to create a selection bias in the flow of information to and among people. As Cass Sunstein argued in his 2002 book *Republic.com,* changing people's beliefs by exposing them to data or alternative arguments is hard to do when they never see or hear those data or arguments and may not even be aware of their existence.[20] Forging meaningful consensus among competing perspectives is not really possible when individuals believe that a majority of others hold views like their own and are dismissive of alternatives. They can come to believe that quite easily, if they only read what people like them read, only hear what people like them enjoy hearing.

The holy grail of commerce—the ability to dig deeply into something you like and not be distracted by noise on the periphery—can be terrible for political consensus building, for learning, and for error correction because it enables individuals to associate only with people with whom they agree and not with those with whom they don't. If you listen only to Fox News and your neighbor listens only to National Public Radio, what kind of a conversation do you think the two of you are going to be able to have?

Affiliative sorting on a global scale is no different. Social psychologists have documented two strong and interconnected tendencies that exist across cultures. When people are asked whether they themselves are biased in their opinions, they say no. When they are asked if they think that *other* people are biased, they say yes. Affiliative sorting in the realm of ideas deeply reinforces this ironic result. At the extreme, "deviant" behaviors look like "normal" behaviors to the people who engage in them, breaking down a key mechanism of social control. People's beliefs become increasingly resistant to change, breaking down a key mechanism of social and political evolution. And people become increasingly subject to manipulation in directions they are already tending, breaking down a key mechanism of reversion to the mean, on which societies rely to constrain extremist behavior, including extremist behavior associated with violence.

There was a moment in the evolution of communications technologies in the 1990s at which, naively, it was common to hear idealistic stories about how the Internet meant the "end of geography." That naiveté should be long gone. Communication networks have their own geography or topology; information systems do not need to be global nor do they need to be open. The notion that "information wants to be free" was wishful thinking. People who use and process information, institutions and devices that connect to communications and transportation networks, thus information itself has boundaries of nationality, religious affiliation, or other separating characteristics that segregate communities to create distinct bodies of knowledge, claims of truth, and calls to action.

Seeing those possibilities for what they really are tells us important things about the evolving shape of the global marketplace of ideas. Understanding these details is not an arcane issue of technological standards or epistemology. It is a prerequisite to successful competition.

Young, urban, and non-Western thinkers. The demography of the population that makes up the global marketplace of ideas is increasingly young, increasingly urban, and—of course—non-Western. What does a population map of the world really look like today? As of 2003, Europeans, Canadians, and Americans together made up just 17 percent of global population. By 2050 they will be 12 percent, perhaps less. The developing world's middle-class population alone—1.2 billion by 2030, a 200 percent increase since 2005—will be greater than the populations of Europe, Canada, the United States, and Japan combined.[21]

Global populations are also becoming more urban. For the first time in history, more than half of the world's population now lives in cities. The rural-to-urban migration trend continues and will accelerate further in the coming decades, by some projections to more than 70 percent by 2050. Urban sub-Saharan Africa will double; China, about 40 percent urban today, will be at 75 percent; India, between 30 percent and 55 percent. Today's megacities like Mumbai (about 20 million), Shanghai (16 million), Cairo and Manila (12 million each), and Lagos (10–14 million) will grow that much larger.[22] Why does this matter? Because the future of world politics and tomorrow's playing field for the global competition of ideas lies in the political economy and sociology of these chaotic, vibrant, pulsing cities of developing Asia, Latin America, and Africa—not the urbane, well-ordered, wealthy, and familiar cities of Western Europe, nor the mythic rural self-sufficient frontier communities of the nineteenth-century American West.

The inhabitants of these developing-world cities are young. Around half the population of Pakistan today is below the age of twenty-four. Lagos is a city dominated by children and teenagers. The math is simple but worth a strong reminder: today's eighteen-year-old was born after 1990. There is no Cold War in her memory. When she thinks of the impact on her life of America's presence in the world, she barely remembers Bill Clinton. Franklin Roosevelt and Harry Truman are curiosities of history, someone else's experience. There are no pictures of John F. Kennedy hanging over sofas in living rooms of apartments in the slums of Jakarta. A discussion of America's post–World War II generosity hardly resonates.

The global marketplace of ideas is increasingly made up of a generation that came of age after 9-11. Some joined in candlelight vigils of support and empathy in the immediate aftermath of 9-11. But a few years later the images from Guantanamo Bay and Abu Ghraib turned empathy and support to enmity and distrust. Those negative images stuck. Americans may think such reactions exaggerated, the images distorted, and the sentiment exploited. But what Americans think isn't the issue. The younger generations abroad do not start from the presumption that the exercise of American power is a force for good in the world. They don't dismiss that possibility, but they are at least skeptical. Yes, many of them wear American-style jeans and some enjoy Hollywood movies. But to extrapolate from that fact that the effect on today's foreign populations of being exposed to unfiltered American culture is, on balance and overall, positive for U.S. policy objectives in the world is wishful thinking. To assume that all of those who are angry and resentful toward America simply misunderstand what America is about, or misinterpret what America means in their lives, is a dysfunctional starting point for policy. Teenagers are not often political leaders—at least not yet or not explicitly—but the generation that will assume greater shares of political power in China, for example, over the next decade also matured long after the post–World War II American moment.

It is simply implausible to believe that the global marketplace of ideas can now or in the future be dominated by the thoughts, needs, arguments, and desires of older men educated in or influenced by the Western world. The density of new urban life, particularly in the developing world, is quickly becoming the convergence point for the forces of globalization and their consequences in ideas. Think of it as a massive incubator. To offer up and distribute new ideologies from this incubator is now a problem that can be solved with lightweight and inexpensive capabilities, increasingly available to almost everyone.

So it is equally nostalgic to believe that the global marketplace of ideas is centered in Boston, New York, or Washington; Paris, Berlin, or London; or even in Shanghai, Bangalore, or San Francisco. To the extent that it is located anywhere, its focus is in the cities of the developing world. These cities are quickly becoming the testing ground for new and old boundaries and identities, the transmission belt for beliefs, the birthplace of new ideologies, the laboratory for experimentation with culture, property, human rights, and violence.

Seeing that landscape for what it really is forces forward more difficult questions about who has or will have power over the flow of information and ideas.

Markets relentlessly breed new competition. War is violent and brutal, appalling and awful. That is one of the reasons why wars end. Market competition is insistent and unrelenting, ruthless and inexhaustible, for ideas as much as for any other commodity. It never really ends. It never even slows down that much.

Wars have rules and schemas, patterns of experience across time that include negotiations, cease-fires, and settlements. Market competition just keeps on driving through its own inexorable energy, where rules are made to be broken. It's an uncomfortable reality that capitalist enterprises face every day: there is no time out. There isn't even a long-term sustainable advantage, other than the ability to recreate competitive advantage every day, in the face of new and unfamiliar challenges.

This is another reason why the competition of ideas is more like a marketplace than a war. There may be certain foundational elements in human experience that give shape to the marketplace—perhaps a quest for dignity, a hope for the health of one's children, a belief in something larger than the exigencies of day-to-day existence. And there may not be. We really don't know for certain. But we do know that even where shared elements such as these exist, they can be interpreted and combined and recombined with other ideological elements into an infinite number of variations, many of which are incompatible with each other. The uncomfortable truth is that believers in radical Salafi Jihadism hold a set of ideas that are just as compelling, coherent, and magnetic within their minds as are the ideas of liberal democracy within ours.

In the realm of ideas more profoundly than in economic and certainly military forms of power, the world has passed into what we earlier called a post-American or Copernican reality. No longer does a global majority believe that the alternative to American-led order is chaos. The academic theory of hegemonic stability, which brought with it the not-so-subtle message that challenges to American order carried the risk of landing the world back into a late 1920s beggar-thy-neighbor nightmare, has faded from the research community, and its underlying message has receded from the consciousness of much of the rest of the world as well. Now the door is wide open for others to offer alternative conceptions of order and the accompanying leadership propositions that would move the world in that direction.

Every generation will promise the end of ideology in one form or another, simply because the notion is as attractive to a political entity as a permanent, unchallenged monopoly position would be to a capitalist enterprise. End-of-ideology prophets will always be wrong, but perhaps never quite so wrong as in the next decade. The story is about more than rising powers challenging U.S. leadership. Twentieth-century globalization changed the way many people experience life economically and politically. It swept aside assumptions about particular aspects of social order and the terms of economic production. Rising powers refract those underlying forces in their own ways, and although the mix has been a heady source of ideological ferment, it is very possibly marginal compared to what might be coming next. Here are two likely ingredients of the coming ferment.

Consider first the ongoing unbundling of what was once called Westphalian sovereignty. States, or governance institutions that aspired to be states, were at one time supposed to have (or at least seek) a territorially bounded, legitimate monopoly on the use of violence. This monopoly was linked to autonomy of formal decision rights against which no supranational organizing principle or rule could intrude, except by choice of the sovereign. If this was the core organizational idea of international politics in the era we called modernity, the one thing we know for sure is that it is now just one among several competing ideas.

A powerful contending example is an organization like Hezbollah, which offers a distinct, rebundled package of religious ideology and promises of salvation, schools, clean water, and rebuilding services for war-damaged homes. It does not aspire to sovereign status, however, and it is uninterested in owning a state or seeking autonomy from others. Joshua Cooper Ramo provocatively but tellingly writes of Hezbollah's "management secrets," its "capacity for creativity and innovation . . . to shift and learn and change," from which much can be distilled analytically without condoning any of its means or ends.[23] It won't be long before new experiments in bundling emerge for which the barriers to entry are lower still—for example in virtual worlds on the Internet. Some of these experiments will be trivial and cartoonish; others will be quite serious. What determines the difference is not corroboration by academic experts or even state leaders that control armies; it is the attractiveness of these organizing ideas to the people who may choose to sign up for them.

Consider also the likely next set of technology innovations. Globalization in the second half of the twentieth century was a big deal. Led by transportation, information, and communications technologies, it remade markets and shook up politics in profound and sometimes unforeseen ways. Yet it did not change, in the deepest sense, what it means to be human. Technologies now emerging in the life sciences touch much more profound parts of life.

It's not science fiction to recognize that we are not just moving goods, services, and money across political boundaries anymore. We are building technologies that may someday redefine life—including gender, sexuality, mortality, disease, and the very boundaries of the human species. What this means for medicine, for ecosystems, and for national power are profound but as yet unanswerable questions. What is more certain is that this kind of change will create unprecedented, almost unimaginable fodder upon which new ideologies may feed. Are we ready to compete in that kind of marketplace?

The United States needs to decide quite soon how it views two different kinds of ideological competition it might face. We need to update a key argument from Walter Lippmann and George Kennan's post–World War II power-balance principles. Kennan famously argued that U.S. global influence did not require domination of all other centers of power.[24] Rather, as long as contenders remained diffuse and separated from each other, rather than allied in a single anti-American consortium, the United States would be secure and influential in the ways that it wanted to be.

The Lippmann/Kennan argument played out well enough in military and economic power. It has pretty consistently held the center of the American foreign policy debate. But do the principles travel well to the realm of ideological competition? More concretely, which of these two scenarios is more threatening to U.S. interests:

A world containing a million scattered conspiracy theories about the United States, none of which really agrees with or even reinforces another? Or a world with a strong and almost single coherent anti-American narrative? If the answer is the former, then policy makers should prepare for a world of unfocused, sullen opposition that expresses itself in a thousand different ways. If the answer is the latter, then they must prepare to face a focused, duopolistic competition against a powerful and magnetic alternative to U.S. leadership.

We are not—at least not in this chapter—trying to answer this question for decision makers. Simply posing it suggests the kind of thinking that is needed.

The competition of ideas respects no borders. In this arena, domestic policy and foreign policy truly are one. America has undergone something of a small democratic revolution in the last decade, enabled by the Internet and driven forward by a more openly expressed and fundamental confidence in human beings and their ability to reason together. As a nation the United States has come to privilege and celebrate the value of individuals' personal beliefs, opinions, and assessments of data in the search for that which is meaningful and true. The arguments of experts and pundits are increasingly questioned for their accuracy and objectivity.[25] Citizen journalism, blogs, and the wisdom of the crowd are, depending on the subject matter, considered at least as legitimate as the *New York Times* and other established news sources. We suspect this is more than a temporary fad, because it taps deeply into core elements of American political culture. Alexander Hamilton would not have understood it, but Thomas Jefferson would—and it was Jefferson whose ideas prevailed.

The problem is that U.S. policy has seemed to say that this small revolution mostly stops at America's political borders. When Americans look outside into the rest of the world, and particularly at this moment into the Arab world, they seem (and are seen) to believe and act as if others are somehow less capable of the "small d" democratic discourse that Americans believe in. They seem (and are seen) to deny the individuality inherent in their domestic life to others. Instead Americans want to assert that they can tell others, with intellectual and sometimes even political authority, what is right for them and what they ought to believe—including what they ought to believe about Americans. President Obama's June 2009 Cairo speech launched an effort to change this dynamic, and it was followed up with a number of small but important real impact initiatives. But the persistence of this damaging belief in the face of those positive moves is troubling evidence of how deeply rooted the beliefs have become.

The implications are simple and profound. If human beings living inside the United States have the capability to reason together, then surely human beings in other countries do as well. The alternative claim is really just this stark: that a compelling American message can change the intellectual or emotional valence with which others view the impact of America on their lives. That claim simply is not defensible in the twenty-first century, and policies that rely implicitly or explicitly upon it will fail.

We are digging deeper than democracy promotion. That is a program for institutions, not individuals. Of course there are institutional prerequisites to the effective functioning of social discourse. You obviously can't learn much from coerced conversation, and a censored opinion if never heard does not have a chance to convince anyone of anything. We are talking instead about a more foundational reality: Whatever you may believe about the efficacy of soft power, soft power is much harder to fake than hard power. Throughout history, militarily weak states have built Potemkin villages of one kind or another to deceive their adversaries about how strong and capable they really were. That worked a lot of the time.

But there are no Potemkin villages for soft power. How we organize ourselves and deliver on our expressed beliefs *at home* is now a fully visible and extremely powerful signal to the rest of the world about the underlying logic of America's global presence. The global competition of ideas is not a war to be fought with a segmented part of our society that is walled off and fed resources from the rest. It is a competition in offering meaning and dignity to others. That, by its nature, engages a whole society.

George W. Bush was right when he said that our struggle is the struggle of a generation. But he was wrong in his limited understanding of what that really meant for the

United States. Barack Obama has a different and to our eyes a more appropriate view of the landscape. But even his administration hasn't grappled with the broader consequences.

Add it all up. For the moment, at least, the playing field for the global competition of ideas is anything but flat and fair. It is tilted in very important ways *against* the United States. If there is any reasonable definition of "anti-Americanism" as a structural feature of world politics, this is it. Can any idea right now that is, or is seen as, coming out of the United States arrive on the global marketplace and compete without being heavily discounted by many in many parts of the world from the moment it appears? At this moment, we think the answer is no. The election of Barack Obama softened that effect, but it certainly did not eliminate it.

American ideas are still delegitimated to a meaningful degree simply because they are seen as being American or are promoted by the United States. In the Middle East just now, and in significant slices of other geographies as well, a pro-American government is often assumed to be a corrupt government. The United States gets more than its fair share of blame for failures of global governance and underprovision of global public goods. American power is often thought to inherently, almost necessarily, cause injustice and humiliation to others, particularly (but not uniquely) Muslims.

This is not good news for the United States. But no news is as challenging as this simple summary insight. In 2010, globally, there remains a deep skepticism about the proposition that the United States can be more powerful and the world can be a better place at the same time. The belief that these two things could be consistent or even reinforce each other was the most valuable and precious advantage America had in the post–World War II global milieu. It has eroded, and that changes the nature of ideological competition dramatically. A new foreign policy leadership proposition has to find a way to put that belief back in play. A good way to start is to take to heart what Oliver Wendell Holmes called "the best test of truth": "the power of the thought to get itself accepted in the competition of the market."[26]

3

FORGING A JUST SOCIETY

Go back for a moment to the big ideas that defined U.S. foreign policy in the second half of the twentieth century—that peace was better than war, hegemony better than balance of power, capitalism better than socialism, democracy better than dictatorship, and Western culture better than anything else. Foreign policy thinkers in the United States today aren't blind to the fact that questions have been raised about each of these ideas, especially when the ideas are thought about one at a time. In fact, the notion that each big idea taken singly is subject to debate has become almost mainstream now, to the point where many efforts to contribute to the debate are really just attempts to state more eloquently what are by now familiar arguments. Most often that is done to defend the resilience and continued relevance of each twentieth-century big idea in the face of what looks like (but isn't really) fundamental resistance.

That's not good enough. The challenges to the five big ideas of the twentieth century are much more profound when taken together and create a different and considerably more difficult reality. What looks like fundamental resistance to all five is, in fact, what it appears to be. The United States has not confronted, either intellectually or politically, the deep consequences of that reality. The twenty-first century will not be an ideological rerun of the half-century after World War II. Recasting, rewording, and remessaging with the intention of restoring the power of the old synthesis has run its course.

As we said in Chapters 1 and 2, the new playing field is a self-consciously Copernican world with a marketplace of ideas where TINA simply is not enough. It needs a new leadership proposition. We believe a distinctly American, globally competitive, forward leaning, hopeful, and effective leadership proposition can be built up from two fundamental ingredients—a just society and a world order. The first, a just society, is the subject of this chapter.

What Is a Just Society on a Global Stage?

When it comes to promoting just societies around the world, Americans have a few things to unlearn and forget before making use of their society's and state's fundamental strengths of justice on a global stage. These include much of what is "known" about American exceptionalism, ideology, and the relationship between process and power. We will have to examine closely some relatively unexamined "truths" about democracy. And we will have to modify and modernize what comes close for many Americans to a foundational belief: "That government is best which governs least."

In fact none of these arguments and beliefs are indispensable or even central to what is most American and most attractive about a leadership proposition that promises progress toward a just society globally. They are simply instrumental beliefs, a particular moment's way of implementing more fundamental propositions about how human beings can and ought to combine together so that the whole is greater than the sum of the parts. Even if that moment lasted for half a century or more inside the United States, its consequences for institutions and policy were never appropriate for much of the globe. Although those instrumental beliefs need to be honored as a historical moment, they do not need to be brought back and restored to their former supposed glory. The challenge we face is to adapt the more fundamental propositions about just societies to the demands of today's and tomorrow's world.

What is a just society and how do you know if you live in one? Thankfully, a leadership proposition for international politics doesn't need to answer this timeless question comprehensively; it only needs to represent a position that demanders of justice can respect. If we strip away the philosophical, legal, and theological complexities just for a moment, there are a few core points that are robust across cultures and countries.

Here's a simple starting point. A just society is a place where things and persons are properly ordered in relation to one another, and where the people who make up the society perceive this to be the case. A just society is one in which people can see the institutions of the society work, since the ordering of people and things is precisely what institutions do. It doesn't sound like a very high bar, does it? But in practice a remarkably small slice of humanity lives within societies that cross that bar at any given moment. Add a dynamic element—where you ask institutions to work over time and to manage change—and the threshold moves further upward. But a dynamic element is precisely what the present historical moment of rapid change demands. So let's add a couple of additional requirements that capture that reality.

A just society is one whose institutions work, and are seen to work, to promote the goals and aspirations of the individuals and the collective of individuals that make up a society. A just society is one that endures, because justice can only exist in a meaningful way if it lasts over some considerable period of time. It is one that learns, because if justice derives from the goals and aspirations of human beings, it will never be a static concept but will always be in the course of updating itself to changed circumstances. And a just society is one that can expand to include new members, that is open to new adherents who wish to sign up for the bargain or social contract. Such openness is increasingly important in a world of porous boundaries, enhanced mobility, and societal heterogeneity. With that list of requirements, it's a pretty tall order.

What to Let Go and What to Keep

The first thing Americans need to unlearn about just societies on a global stage is how their notions of justice inside the United States are affected by the U.S. environment of plenty. It may not always feel like it in the last few years, but the United States really did win the geopolitical lottery in material abundance and security. Such an environment has made Americans more than a little parochial when it comes to understanding the harsh realities that other societies face when they confront tough choices around justice.

Two oceans separated the United States from the empires of Europe and Asia in the eighteenth and nineteenth centuries. They still did so in the twentieth century—even with the advent of strategic airpower. Not a single American alive today has ever experienced foreign troops carrying out a physical invasion of his or her homeland. The notion of being surrounded by enemies or potential enemies is an abstract one that might resonate logically but not emotionally, the way it does for others on the planet. Pearl Harbor was an attack on an island territory, not even yet a state, thousands of miles off the coast of California, and it happened almost seventy years ago. The terrorist attacks on the World Trade Center were deeply traumatic but would not be unfamiliar or unprecedented in the experience of many other countries.

The anxiety some Americans feel about immigration from Mexico and the occasional spillover from mostly drug- and gang-related violence is the exception that proves the point. These are certainly real security concerns for the United States. But a threat to core security needs, sovereignty, the core institutions that support U.S. efforts to create a just society at home? Not even close. America spent most of its history creating the infrastructure for a just society at home without having to worry too much about the destructive impact of external forces.

When it comes to material abundance Americans' luck was at least as good. The continent was set up for extraordinary agricultural productivity. It had excellent natural navigation routes; enormous deposits of iron, coal, uranium, oil, and natural gas. The list could also include hydro, solar, and wind for energy sources; vineyard-ready climate and soil for productive agriculture; a vast amount of physical space to accommodate industry and immigration; and forests above ground and rock formations below that can be transformed into carbon sinks. Americans may intellectually understand the notion of resource shortages, but American society has never really experienced what it means to lack access to a natural resource necessary for survival.

Neither geographical advantage nor ample resources make building a just society simple. But would you rather try to do it in a vast desert, on a flood plain, or on top of mountainous hardscrabble terrain that cannot grow food?

The second thing Americans need to unlearn is the exceptionalism of settled formulas. There is no single solution to building a just society. You can't find it in the U.S. Constitution, the *Federalist Papers,* or in the works of John Rawls, Plato, John Maynard Keynes, Jeremy Bentham, or Martin Luther King, Jr. Each generation's prophet trumpeting the "end of history" notwithstanding, there never will be a settled formula for a just society that people can simply implement and follow. The building of a just society is always a process, an ongoing debate in which the striving is as important as anything else.

Americans know that, don't they? Yes, they do. In a sense they know it so well that often process is placed ahead of outcomes. In other words, Americans have sometimes talked themselves into believing that a just society is a democratic one, a place where voters make choices at the ballot box. When pressed, they acknowledge that more may be needed, but it often remains both a starting and an ending point anyway.

That's not good enough for a global stage. Democracy is its own settled formula. It is a process, not an outcome. It is a set of rules for allocating power, not a set of rules for allocating human needs. And it is a fixed set of rules as well. Here's where the two "unlearnings" come together. In much of the world (outside the wealthier countries in particular), there is very little constituency for process and quite a lot more for concrete outcomes. For much of the world it is really this simple: that government is best which governs best. People in countries with mass poverty, prevalent disease, and other pressing human needs are looking to be protected not just from government and from power but also by government and given some of what they need by power. Legitimacy depends on performance, not just process. Whether government is less or more, big or small is not so important; what matters is whether government helps provide for human needs or fails to do so.

To privilege process over outcomes is a luxury that most human beings on this planet can't afford just now.

That's not to say process is irrelevant, because human be-ings everywhere are quite smart enough to recognize that the two are connected in some fashion over time. And of course it is important to keep in mind that getting pro-cesses right helps protect against repression. But it is to say that to the extent Americans advocate democracy for others as a core component of a just society, it needs to be a vision of democracy that delivers what others want for themselves, and not what Americans think they want for them. A regionwide poll in Latin America a few years ago found a majority preferring "a return to dictatorship if it would bring economic benefits." Fifty-eight percent agreed that leaders should go "beyond the law" if neces-sary for the social good. Fifty-six percent gave higher pri-ority to economic development than to democracy.[1] This is not some kind of parochial leftist sentiment. "If any-thing can change the pessimistic attitude of many Latin Americans toward democracy," wrote Mario Vargas Llosa, noted Peruvian author and conservative former presiden-tial candidate, "it is an improvement in justice."[2]

Janice Stein of the University of Toronto once said that the great American pathology of the 1990s was a toxic combination of complacency and arrogance that led us to "normalize the abnormal" when it came to critical ele-ments of leading a just society. She's tough, but (mostly) right. Think of some of the surreal assumptions that de-veloped over the course of that lucky decade:

When technology empowered those who could take ad-
    vantage of decentralization, Americans told them-
    selves that everyone would be included, and that tech-

nology would damage unfriendly governments but empower friendly ones.

When the U.S. economy soared on the back of various finance bubbles that were driven largely by excess Chinese savings, Americans told themselves this was incontrovertible evidence of the superiority of the U.S. innovation machine and growth ecology.

Although the U.S. government asked global multilateral institutions to provide public goods to the international system, they increasingly cut contributions—financial, political, and ideological—to their support and foundations.

Americans deregulated sectors of their economy as a function of ideology as much as a function of data and metrics about what was happening as a result.

What the United States had once promoted as economic development aimed at enhancing prosperity with justice and equality was narrowed to human capital investment that enables countries to compete in global markets. Those important elements of justice and equality fell by the wayside.

Americans thought the worldwide demand for liberal democracy was more fundamental and more heartfelt than for anything else, even for justice. When probed on that issue, Americans retreated to the assertion that the two were basically the same and always mutually reinforcing.

Several wars and an unprecedented global economic crisis later, Americans can and should suffer a bit of a confidence deficit. That's a healthy change. If it creates some lasting humility, that will go a long way toward restoring the world's willingness to hear a new proposition from America about leadership in global social justice.

We need to be clear, though, about what we mean when we say "willingness to hear." For most of the last decade, many around the world would simply discount much of what Washington said about global leadership, seeing it as prima facie self-serving or so imbued with a parochial ideology as to be insulting. A newly found willingness to hear a proposition is not the same as a readiness to accept it, and certainly not to do so without serious bargaining. There is no better demonstration of this wariness than the complicated reactions across the Islamic world to President Obama's June 2009 speech in Cairo. The content of the speech and Obama's charisma made the "mutual respect" pledge credible and the offer of a "new beginning" attractive. A new beginning, though, is just that. What comes next? Will the relationship contribute more to fostering just societies in the Arab and Islamic world than in the past?

In this case but also more globally, we believe that America could offer to the world an attractive new leadership proposition. Such a proposition for a just society would contain four critical elements: autonomy, opportunity, protection, and heterogeneity.

What the United States Should Offer to the World

Autonomy. One irreducible ingredient of an American leadership proposition is autonomy—the right of individuals to decide for themselves what it is that they want. Within this we need to make clear what is often a subtle but critical distinction between individualism and individuality. "I am out for myself, society benefits, and even if it doesn't I should be able to be out for myself" is the basic proposition of extreme individualism. Ayn Rand's version of the heroic encapsulates this logic. Individuality has a different valence. "I am myself and society benefits from each of us fulfilling our uniqueness" is the core logic of individuality. Let me be myself but more in ways that express my persona than demand full freedom of action. There is within this subtle difference more recognition of the societal context that enables individuals to pursue their individuality. The autonomy of the individual is interdependent with societal context and consequences.

A few years ago one of us was at a Chinese university developing joint programs. During a break a guide showed me around the grounds. We walked past a beautiful grassy quad that was roped off. "American students lie out sunbathing and run around playing Frisbee on their quads," I commented. "There are too many of us," she responded. "We have to stay off." My initial reaction was to perceive yet another example of restricted individual rights. But as I thought about it, I realized there also was a sense of societal responsibility.

Those that do want to play Frisbee no doubt find ways to do so. Roping off a grassy quad is nothing like jailing and killing dissidents. The Chinese fully understand the difference. Many Americans today believe and assert that an (apparently silent) majority of Chinese citizens are calling, quietly but determinedly, for democracy against the wishes of the ruling Communist Party. We surely know that there are some, and there likely would be more if not for the regime's repressiveness. But how much real knowledge or data do we have to back up our assumptions?

In much of the Arab world it is personal dignity and social justice more than unfettered individual freedom that are culturally precious. Hamas and Hezbollah gain supporters not just coercively but by providing jobs, health care, and other social services. These are real needs and real aspirations that need to be taken seriously and at face value. The distinction Amartya Sen makes in his book *The Idea of Justice* between sweeping claims of fully just societies and a "results-oriented" approach focusing on tangible progress on gross injustices helps in this regard.[3] The reality is one of discourse among competing conceptions not singular superiority. Once we fully internalize that point, to assert that we understand things about human nature that others do not is not at all promoting the autonomy of individuals to make their own decisions. It's not even respecting what autonomy they might already have in their existing situations. It is certainly not being honest about the internal logic of what it means to grant the respect of autonomy to others.

Sound obvious? Think of how many times the United States has failed to recognize others' autonomy. Since 1984 under Republican presidents, the "global gag rule" made it illegal for any foreign aid organization that receives support from USAID to provide information about abortion to aid recipients, much less to offer actual abortion services. This isn't just bad policy for global health, reproductive rights, and family planning. It's an assault on the autonomy of women in developing countries to make their own decisions about how to manage their bodies. And most of us would agree that determining what each of us wants to do with our sexual lives is a pretty core part of what it means to be autonomous as a human being. Surely it is as fundamental as the right to decide what job we should take or what currency in which to store our assets?

Americans have little trouble demonstrating such autonomy when they talk and act *at home* about their faith in the power of open discourse to enable individuals to make better choices about what they want. Think of the current American fascination with social networks on the Internet—easy to make fun of, but not a passing fad given the amount of time and energy that people devote to these connections. Think of then-president-elect Obama's request to Americans during the holiday season of 2008 that they sit down with their families, friends, and neighbors and have serious conversations about the future of health care in the United States.

We're not saying that the American political process or its power elite has fully grappled with what it means to have an empowered, autonomous population acting behind, through, and occasionally around it. Far from it. A population that might want to engage substantively in collective decision making more often and more deeply than in the episodic trip to the ballot box poses really hard questions for political operatives, most of whom would prefer to be able to mobilize that population on demand only when needed to break an inside-the-Beltway logjam. There is a distinct difference in attitude, however, toward autonomy for Americans and autonomy for those outside U.S. borders. On what possible basis can we deny or even downplay equivalent levels of autonomy for individuals outside the United States? "Their societies are not set up to enable autonomous action," some say. Fine, we say in response. What a great opportunity for a new American leadership proposition to gain traction.

Acting on that potential is not first and foremost about holding elections. Elections are important expressions of autonomy, but the act of voting does not magically confer autonomy on people who don't have it in their lives for the other 364 days of the year. A new American leadership proposition is one that works for all those other days and leads with that contribution rather than with the electoral moment. What does this mean in practice? Things that we actually know how to do and are really quite good at. Let's build open communication platforms by flooding the world with hardware and software that is secure against censorship. Let's give away cell phones and the networks that connect them. Let's put wireless broadband in the foreign aid budget, not just in the domestic stimulus agenda.

In other words, let's use our leading-edge technology capabilities to enhance the autonomy of individuals to decide for themselves—not because technology is a silver bullet but because it helps. In so doing the United

States would demonstrate its faith that even if those decisions are not pro-American in their particulars, they will eventually benefit the things Americans care about in the world. That's an incredibly powerful statement to others about leadership, because it gives up control and substitutes for it a deep and abiding confidence in the ability of autonomous individuals to express their needs and desires. The expression of such confidence is one important version of what democracy is fundamentally about.

Opportunity. A second irreducible ingredient of an American leadership proposition is opportunity—the removal of roadblocks that stand in the way of political and economic empowerment for those who seek it. This has got to sound at least as obvious. Isn't opportunity the essence of America's shared identity? Isn't it what Thomas Jefferson meant when he wrote "life, liberty, and the pursuit of happiness"? We think it is, and we think it is a powerful leadership proposition to offer to the rest of the world.

Leaders who would advance opportunity must first discover what stands in the way. What creates roadblocks between autonomy and empowerment? In today's world there is a single presumptive answer to that question. It's an answer that would not satisfy a serious political theorist, but it would make intuitive and practical sense to a vast majority of the world's population. It is simply this: impenetrable concentrations of power.

When some people or some institutions have sufficient power that they can deny it to others and be confident of the fact that they can do so over time, then opportunity

suffers in a fundamental way. That's the place to inter-
vene. An American leadership proposition about opportunity should be about making impenetrable concentrations of power penetrable again.

That's part of the motivation behind the fascination
with elections—when elections work they do part of what
is prescribed by inserting at least an element of uncertainty into the future of those who have power today. But
there are other ways of undermining impenetrable concentrations of power that show more immediate results,
that have the same or greater impact, and that the United
States can and should help others to learn to use.

Antitrust regulation and law, for example, is one domain in which breaking impenetrable concentrations of
power has created a greater social good. This isn't about
some arcane legal or economic reasoning. The argument
we should be making to the world is this: antitrust is neither just a business issue nor a problem of capitalism. It's
a key ingredient of building just societies.

Monopolies do more than undermine economic efficiency, innovation, and fair pricing in markets. Monopolies are a problem of social justice because monopolies almost by definition create roadblocks to individuals'
ability to pursue opportunity. You can see what a concentration of power in markets does to prices; what is sometimes a bit harder to see but at least as important is what
those concentrations of power do to squash potential
competition. And since a real monopoly almost has to see
the opportunities that belong to others as a potential
source of competition across some spectrum of action,

the squashing is sooner or later locked in as something monopolies will do. Business monopolies will do it in markets. And other kinds of institutions, including international organizations and nongovernmental organizations (NGOs), will do it in their own way.

How would the principles of antitrust law translate in the practice of leading a just society? We can start with markets, where it's a bit more straightforward. The United States should replace many of our election observers with experts in antitrust regulation and law. Some of the technical assistance provided to promote democracy could be replaced by technical assistance to implement antitrust systems in emerging economies.

The actions of these antitrust programs will certainly cause pain for American companies operating in the developing world. U.S. acceptance of such consequences adds real credibility to a sacrifice for the sake of leadership. It would serve also as an important corrective to the myth that a "rising tide lifts all boats," which has been considered part and parcel of globalization for roughly the last two decades. Any decent economist knows that economic change creates winners and losers as a matter of course.

The serious version of the argument was to claim that globalization would bring increased wealth for the world as a whole—and that argument was probably right. Standard economic theory then states that the new wealth created is sufficient for winners to compensate losers and still come out ahead. That's also right, so far as it goes. But look closely: the economic logic says that winners *can* compensate losers (and still come out ahead); not that they *will* in fact choose to do so. If they don't believe they have to redistribute some of the winnings in order to keep the system going, or if they feel no moral compunction to do so, or if they never really see the losers lose because they are living far away, or any number of other reasons including just simple greed, then globalization can at once create unprecedented wealth and leave in its wake extreme poverty for the world as a whole.

Even within the United States' domestic borders, social mobility has declined along with a rise in income and wealth, a disparity that now places us at the highest level of inequality among developed nations. The less successful parts of American society have seen by some measures an absolute fall in their standard of living during the last two decades—even before the financial crisis of 2008–2009. In the minds and in the lives of many, income disparity in America is coming awfully close to signaling impenetrable concentrations of power that will self-reinforce through generations, permanently locking out some classes.

If this seems leftish, think Madison not Marx. His warning in the tenth essay in *The Federalist Papers* about the danger of "factions" reads presciently about the contemporary K Street interest group complex. "The friend of popular governments never finds himself so much alarmed for their character and fate as when he contemplates their propensity to this dangerous vice" [factions] . . . The instability, injustice and confusion introduced into the public councils have, in truth, been the mortal diseases under which popular governments have everywhere perished."[4] Madison posits how the system he and fellow Founders were constructing would check against factions. It's doubtful he would be as sanguine if he went online to *Politico* today. If Americans were to open up opportunity at home and take a parallel set of actions abroad, they would supply the second core ingredient of a proposition to lead a just society.

Protection. The third irreducible ingredient of our leadership proposition is protection—creating and ensuring safety for people who are made vulnerable by change. If you had to develop a single simple way to measure the level of justice a society provides, you could do worse than to ask, "How consistently does this society protect its most vulnerable members from harm that is not under their control?" That metric has a strong ethical basis, of course. But it has a terrifically practical basis as well—since in a period of rapid and unpredictable change, any one of us could be in an intense state of vulnerability at any moment and want for ourselves precisely that protection.

Let's make an even stronger statement. The importance of protection doesn't have to be the product of Rawls's veil of ignorance at some imaginary moment called the "original position."[5] It is now a stark reality of modern life in an interconnected world, a product of a kind of clear-headed certainty that either we or those we know will be vulnerable at some point.

This is why the debacle of New Orleans after Hurricane

Katrina was more than just a humanitarian disaster in-side the United States. It was a foreign policy debacle of the first order, on a par with the government's failure to plan for the post–"mission accomplished" political and security landscape in Iraq. Why? Because Katrina illus-trated the abject failure of the U.S. government to pro-tect a vulnerable population even at home, where it is lo-gistically the easiest; where votes matter; where victims speak English; where TV cameras, cell phone snapshots, and YouTube videos are everywhere. That America didn't plan for New Orleans smacks of incompetence and indif-ference. That the government couldn't mobilize quickly and aggressively enough to compensate for that lack of planning suggests a fundamental shortfall of capabili-ties. Those messages went out to the rest of the world in real time, in the form of pictures and video, showing an economically disadvantaged and predominantly African-American population left to scavenge for food, water, and in some cases, survival.

A month after Katrina, one of us was talking with a prominent Indian general-diplomat. "I am a friend of the United States," he said. "I don't always agree with all your policies but believe that the world needs your leadership. What, though, am I supposed to tell my people about Hurricane Katrina? In our part of the world natural di-sasters hit all the time; plenty of tsunamis, not just the 2004 one that grabbed the world's attention. For us the most basic responsibility of government is to help people in such situations. How much of a model of democratic governance can you be when you did so little for people in need in your own country?"

A Singaporean newspaper columnist put it similarly: "We were shocked at what we saw. Death and destruction from natural disaster is par for the course. But the pictures of dead people left uncollected on the streets, armed looters ransacking shops, survivors desperate to be rescued, racial divisions—these were truly out of synch with what we'd imagined the land of the free to be, even if we had encountered homelessness and violence on visits there . . . If America became so unglued when bad things happen in its own backyard, how can it fulfill its role as leader of the world?"[6] If the U.S. government isn't serious about protecting vulnerable populations in New Orleans, how much less likely is it to do anything for the vulnerable people of Darfur, Mexico, Pakistan, or Bangladesh?

A practical part of a new American leadership proposition around protection of the vulnerable must acknowledge that many of the global systems on which life today depends—both natural and manmade—are stretched close to the breaking point, even when they seem on the surface to be working tolerably well. There is so little excess capacity and redundancy in these systems that it only takes a small shock to drive them far out of equilibrium and into something resembling catastrophic failure. No single precise shock is predictable. The fact that there will be such shocks is nearly certain. And we know from theory and experience that tightly coupled systems with little backup capacity, when stretched the way we've now stretched them, will fail and fail catastrophically at unpredictable but not infrequent intervals. This is the phenomenon famously called "normal accidents" by Charles Perrow.[7]

Rapid and massive inflation in the price of food (the so-called agflation episode of 2007–2008) is an example of that fact. It took just a little excess pressure on the global food supply chain, a bit of bad weather, and a moderate increase in demand for biofuel feedstocks to transform what might have otherwise been a gradual rise in food prices into a rapid and radical price shock, which was reversed in similarly radical fashion when the global credit crisis hit.

The 2010 Deepwater Horizon oil spill is another example, an all too tragic one. That accidents happen when drilling a mile deep is perhaps unsurprising. Some measures could have been taken to make it less likely, but nothing could have been assuredly preventive. The failures were in the shocking incapacity to contain the accident. We didn't have the right tools in the toolkit, the British Petroleum CEO offhandedly explained. Why not? BP sure had plenty of tools in its toolkit for exploiting the oil, for marketing it, for lobbying in Washington and Baton Rouge for a light-on-safety regulatory environment. Safety priorities are not inherent to the enterprise: they reflect choices made and policy environments promulgated. Norway has a Petroleum Safety Authority as an independent body with substantial authority for ensuring safety and also emergency preparedness. It still manages to reap substantial profits and fill its sovereign wealth fund while not having its fjords tarred, its fishermen lose their livelihood, and its wildlife face extinction. Ultimately it too is subject to the law of normal accidents, but policies can lower the likelihood of occurrence and raise the capacity for containing the effects. In this regard the Obama administration was rightly criticized for not having strengthened the regulatory environment prior to the crisis and especially for its slow and piecemeal response once the crisis hit.

It is nearly certain that these and other kinds of accidents will become more frequent in the next decade, and possibly much more frequent. It is fully certain that media coverage of the human suffering will be widespread, instantaneous, and global. A compelling American leadership proposition for just societies would be something like this—to pursue policies at home ensuring that safety and emergency response tools are parts of corporate toolkits, making the United States more leader than laggard in environmental protection, and to allocate by law 5 or 10 percent of the U.S. defense budget to rapid emergency response capabilities for postdisaster relief abroad. It was commonplace to point to U.S. aid after the 2004 Asian tsunami as one of the most important success stories of the Bush administration's foreign policy. Commonplace, and correct. Sustained capability and commitment to protect the vulnerable would be an even more compelling demonstration of a new U.S. leadership proposition.

Heterogeneity. The fourth key element is making our own societal heterogeneity a source of vitality that strengthens us at home and is truly exemplary in a world in which differences of individual and group identity breed so much fear of "the other." This is even more challenging today than in the past (and it was more challenging then than some of our myths recount). It has to be done amid immigration demagoguery and persistent racial and ethnic inequalities. And it has to be done with many more "pluribuses" out of which to forge *E pluribus unum.*

In 1957, when the segregationist governor of Arkansas was blocking integration of the public schools, President Eisenhower sent in the National Guard partly out of concern about how the denial of basic civil rights at home would play in the Cold War ideological competition, especially in the Third World. In one respect this was the exercise of classic soft power in Joseph Nye's sense of "entice and attract." It also was the move of a shrewd realist. The Cold War struggle, Hans Morgenthau observed, ultimately would be determined "by the visible virtues and vices of their [U.S., Soviet] respective political, economic and social systems . . . It is at this point that foreign policy and domestic politics merge . . . The United States ought to again concentrate its efforts upon creating a society at home which can again serve as a model for other nations to emulate."[8] What was true then is truer now.

Understanding the Competitors

Human beings will always compete among themselves to define what is a just society. The most ambitious competitors will define a plausible winner in that competition as one whose ideas have universal applicability, those that can work for everyone. And then—if they are relatively tolerant and enlightened—they will acknowledge that concepts and practices other than theirs have some positive aspects but eventually will fail as competitive leadership propositions because they don't have supposedly universal applicability. Or it may be that they don't solve all the problems that existing concepts of justice have solved, or they have some other shortcomings.

Here's how Americans tend to fall prey to this pathology. They may idealize some purported competitors, recognize that American concepts of justice are not the only game in town, and then just as quickly rationalize away the competition by painting it as parochial.

One example can be found in Americans' attitudes toward northern European social democracies. For some, the most compelling examples of just societies can be found in places like Denmark and Sweden (often, it's worth noting, extolled by Americans who have spent precious little time living in those places). But a competitor for ideological leadership on a global stage? Hardly possible. Doesn't justice in these societies depend on their being both small and rich? Doesn't it depend (sadly) on their relative ethnic homogeneity and de facto insulation from foreigners with different ideas? Aren't they built on an obsolescing economic model that relies on government taking an excessive proportion of GDP in taxes? Can't they only get away with it because of wealth accumulated in previous generations, ironically through conquest and colonialism? Doesn't this all lead to stifled innovation and a "museum culture" that lacks vibrancy and spark? There's no leadership proposition here that's relevant to aspiring, developing states and societies around the world that weren't born to advantage. Right?

Americans have been similarly intrigued yet dismissive of Singapore, a small, rich, peaceful, benevolent regime in South Asia that achieved independence, rule of law, global economic integration, and profound "Westernization" in business practices. It did so in little more than two generations, growing from a per capita GDP more like Nigeria's to one that rivals America's. Americans who visit Singapore find it delightfully clean, orderly, efficient, and politely welcoming from the moment they step off the plane into the ultra-modern Singapore airport. They sense the energy of a developmental ideology that now points to information and biotechnology as the leading edges of innovative growth. They later hear aspiring leaders in many other places, from Saudi Arabia to South Africa, talk about Singapore as the model they'd like to emulate. Maybe as an economy. But as a just society? It seems inconceivable. Americans understand that Singapore is certainly rich, peaceful, and orderly. They also understand that it is a near-dictatorship. It lacks press freedom and the right to criticize the state. It depends heavily on migrant labor to do the scut work that native Singaporeans reject. Day-to-day life has all the excitement of a suburban shopping mall. To put it bluntly, if justice is this boring, who really wants it that badly? The example of Singapore can't possibly be an attractive leadership proposition to very many others. Right?

Wrong. When the "universal applicability" argument says that a viable ideological competitor must have broad and deep applicability around the world in order to gain real traction, it makes three important errors. The first is to assume that ideological leadership is like an idealized scientific theory, that it must explain everything that previous theories explained plus more in order to replace an existing theory.[9] But that's not the way it actually works in most scientific debates, regardless of how it is expected to work. A new leadership proposition doesn't have to be better than an old one along every dimension to get people's attention. It just needs to appeal to something they really care about.

The second error embeds the assumption that the old American leadership proposition was and is, in some fashion, itself comprehensive, and therefore that competitors must be at least as comprehensive in order to matter. It's not and never was. The American just society argument of the late twentieth century had a very strong position on market-based economics but almost no position on the natural environment. It put voting rights at the center and health rights at the periphery (so far at the periphery that the term *health rights* sounds foreign to most Americans). That doesn't need to be taken as a criticism; it's just a recognition that nothing in this realm is complete. Ideological propositions always have blind spots, and fewer blind spots is not always better than more.

The third error is the notion that a serious leadership proposition must have a clearly articulated end state to which it points. In other words, it must possess a logical extension of its story that extends toward some imagi-

nary equilibrium at which its core commitments are re-
vealed. We have all heard this counterexample: anarchism
is a self-limiting ideology because it knows only what it
stands against, not what it stands for, and offers no stable
end state in which its promises are realized. Whether that
is a fair assessment of anarchist thought is not the point;
the criticism is inaccurate. And so are analogous criti-
cisms of radical Islam. The fact that an ideology does not
include an equilibrium end-state claim does not mean
that human beings will reject it.

Maybe this fascination with end states is a leftover
from the days of Marxist utopian thinking. Maybe it is a
genetically or emotionally conditioned attraction to "end
of history" claims. Maybe it is just a Freudian urge toward
Thanatos. Maybe Westerners sometimes see the world of
human beings as a set of engineering problems that a set
of engineered solutions can bring to a conclusive solution. Whatever it is, it blinds us to the importance of
competitive claims on progress toward a notion of a just
society that people find magnetic—even if we don't think
they should.

The most poignant contemporary example for many
Americans comes, of course, from China. A critical question for any American foreign-policy thinker at present is
this: what kind of a challenge, if any, does China pose
to American global interests? As we said in Chapter 1,
the parameters of debate around that question are relatively concrete and predictable, within boundaries, for
economic and military power. It's much less predictable

and much more open when it comes to ideological competition. Does China offer a just society leadership proposition compelling enough to attract and keep followers, in a way that matters for U.S. power and international position?

Consider what citizens of a lower quartile developing country might experience when they listen to the Chinese story. They will hear an argument for using government authority to powerfully set the terms of bargaining that make up social, economic, and political life. State determination should trump self determination and individual political rights. The explanation will be that the role of the state is to govern inside national borders and to bargain in the international sphere with other states for national advantage. And that requires state authority.

They will hear a critique of Western liberal internationalism that posits notions like political conditionality on development aid and the responsibility to protect as simply representing power games perpetuating colonialism. They may be told that these are cynical efforts to define as global and universal what is purely the product of a particular culture that rests on a declining power base.[10] Where, exactly, is this thing that Westerners call "global civil society," and what has it done lately to make your life better? They will hear a defense of deep respect for national autonomy. States ought to deal with each other over business and trade arrangements, not interfere with each others' electoral laws, cultural policies, press freedoms, or religious traditions. What on earth do those

Americans mean when they talk about the "moral reliability" of democracy?

They will be reminded of Deng Xiaoping proclaiming that "to get rich is glorious." They'll be shown the evidence of a country that by this definition has covered itself in historically unprecedented glory by raising hundreds of millions of people out of poverty and into a middle class in just a generation or two. If they listen closely they will hear a further argument, that this kind of wealth achievement is not just a matter of economics but more fundamentally a matter of human dignity, individual fulfillment, and even self-expression. One man, one vote might sound good to some; but one man, one cell phone and enough to eat sounds even better to many others.

The Chinese example offers these: Economic growth that enhances the material well-being of the poor—offered as a substitute rather than a stimulant of demand for political opening. State authority that delivers growth and manages the interface of the nation with global systems and the shocks that sometimes come from them. Institutions that protect the dignity of deeply held nationalist feelings. Improved standards of living and health through mass production consumer goods and generic drugs.

Do you think this sounds like a just society leadership proposition? A substantial number of people on this planet do, and probably will continue to do so. The comparative speed with which the Chinese economy recovered from the financial disasters of 2008–2009 will be another data point that supports this view. To be sure, China does have its own internal problems and tensions—plenty of them, and seemingly increasing in scope and depth. These tarnish the model and may even undermine it. But just as one company cannot count on another company's failings to ensure its competitive market position, so too the United States (and others) cannot count on China's own failings as the basis for their positioning in the global competition of ideas.

Moreover, it is not only governments that are in this competition for leadership. When it comes to promoting just societies, powerful competitors are emerging also in the NGO realm, notably among the cast of what we call "megaphilanthropies." It's a common parlor game to compare the assets of the Gates Foundation to the assets of entire countries—an overstatement really since the foundation's endowment hovers around 35 billion dollars. But economic power is not what really makes a philanthropy "mega" from an international politics perspective.

Rather like the threshold that sets off a superpower country from a mere great power, megaphilanthropies are distinguished by the roles they take on, as much or more than by the size of their bank accounts or capabilities. We used to say that for an astonishing number of people around the world, the first question they asked when they woke up in the morning was, "What is the United States going to do today?" because that was the most important variable affecting the quality of their lives. Over the next decade, it's likely that many people around the world will worry first about what the Gates Foundation is going to do and only then about what the U.S. government is going to do—for exactly the same reason.

We know that foundations, unlike governments, don't like to think of themselves as particularly political actors.[11] Many people who choose to work in globally oriented philanthropy believe they are above politics. The latest generation of business leaders who have entered the philanthropy business cast their organizations' role as an efficiency-seeking machine that measures, manages, and generates value in concrete achievements for social good that transcends politics. Academic analysts unintentionally feed this fancy by labeling these organizations "nongovernmental organizations" or "nonstate actors," which tells you what they are not rather than what they are and thus makes it easy to imagine that megaphilanthropies somehow operate in a secondary political tier below the real players. If that is true, they cannot seriously compete with governments and great powers for social justice leadership on a global scale.

But it is not true. The Gates Foundation is at least as geopolitically important as many of the states it works in, through, and with. Look at who runs public health systems in substantial parts of sub-Saharan Africa. Look at who provides clean water and medicine. Look at the official reception that Bill and Melinda Gates get whenever they travel in recipient states. Whether they choose to talk about themselves explicitly as leaders in promoting just societies, the megaphilanthropies are going to be seen that way by others—and soon enough, we suspect, quite regularly and explicitly by themselves.

That's not all good news from the megaphilanthropy perspective. Like any other political player, they spawn opposition. Let's be stark about this for a moment: insofar as a megaphilanthropy looks set to achieve goals of reducing disease and inequality or promoting more open societies, there are other important actors in the game who will want the philanthropy to fail. Vladimir Putin makes no bones about wanting to reduce the presence of foreign NGOs in Russian politics, and the Russian Parliament has given him the laws to do it. But there are more subtle cases: The village elder who looks askance at women's health clinics; the ethnic group that feels left out when a megaphilanthropy funds a local industry that a different ethnic group dominates; or those who regard labor and environmental protection as limiting economic growth.

There's an obvious but important point here that any just society leadership proposition needs to acknowledge. Justice is not the same as consensus and peace. Much of the time, political controversy should be seen as a sign of success. A just society is less of a promise than a threat for many incumbents in positions of dominance and power. Any reasonable just society leadership proposition will manufacture losers as well as winners. Of course that is the essence of politics, and those who don't want to own up to that fact and play the game well will see that other players who have less compunction about admitting what game they are really playing will turn their efforts upside down.

A final point about global philanthropy is that it is set to become increasingly global not only in terms of its reach but in terms of its origin. The majority of foundations that have a global reach have up until now been based in the United States. That will not be true ten or probably even five years hence. If today's competition for just society leadership involves mostly American foundations, just wait until the next round of competition includes new and disruptive entrants, the Indian or Saudi megaphilanthropist who decides to bring his or her vision of equality, health, and individual dignity to parts of Africa, the Middle East, or even the slums of Los Angeles and Detroit.

Of course it's not only megaphilanthropies that compete for global leadership on just society grounds. Communications technologies have really changed the game, at the very least by making everyone believe they can be global and by making that proposition surprisingly true for many. Religious movements that put the discourse of justice right up in front are a powerful alternative in many parts of the world. In some cases they can and do capture a free ride from governments that actually provide the concrete, material public goods that a justice story needs as prerequisite. Religious movements often get the credit.

It's their ability to articulate what justice is and how societies, institutions, and individuals should act to promote it that wins support for the religious movements. We have all heard the argument that Hezbollah, its social service provision and justice discourse notwithstanding, simply could not run the Lebanese state if it were given the opportunity to do so. Should we be so sure? Outside observers think this means that Hezbollah does not offer a competitive leadership proposition, because it cannot do all the things that other leaders can (or say they can). That's outside reasoning and does not reflect the reality on the ground. As we said, justice is not like a scientific theory; it needn't prove itself neutral or beneficial across all dimensions to attract adherents. Sometimes the sheer and sole explicitness of calling out justice as its own core ideological commitment is good enough to get people to pay serious attention.

This diversity of opinion reflects a fundamental reality of the Copernican world. The primary dynamic of competition for just society leadership is no longer one of positioning relative to a fixed and central point, the U.S. model—to the extent that it ever really was. Instead, states and societies, NGOs and philanthropies, religions and businesses, and other nascent organizations are self-consciously and self-confidently articulating independent, coherent, eloquent, and consequential notions of what justice is about; and what the correct response of social, political, economic, and spiritual actors to its demands, requirements, and challenges ought to be. It's a wide-open game.

A Legitimate, Just Society

Corporate social responsibility, communications, and image professionals sometimes talk about legitimacy as a form of "permission to play." They mean by this that societies can grant or retract from companies a de facto license to operate in a particular market.

National leaders tend to talk about legitimacy differently, and mostly as a function of their domestic polities. Legitimacy comes from being properly elected, from respecting the constitution, from delivering on promises to your own country. The question of what constitutes legitimacy on the international stage is more fraught. Some talk about legitimacy as respect or admiration, or in a more legalistic tone, legitimacy as a function of your willingness to comply with international law, institutions, and norms.

This has often left the United States playing defense (and never more so than during the Bush years). But we don't need to accept a defensive stance. However you go about getting it, legitimacy can be an exceptional advantage in highly competitive markets. It can play offense as well as defense. If you raise the legitimacy bar high enough, you force your competitors to meet that standard simply to have the right to compete with you on a level playing field.

This is a huge opportunity for an American leadership proposition that puts forward justice as its own core ideological commitment. By "justice" we mean a defensible piece of ideology, with no apologies and no regrets—not secondary to economic growth, rule of law, tolerance, or anything else, as valuable and important (and contributing to just outcomes) as all those things are. Rather, the core commitment of a leadership proposition should be justice for the sake of justice. Such a system would work to promote the goals of individuals and the collective in reasonable balance, endure over time and learn as it goes, and expand to include new members as they wish to subscribe. Is that something the United States can authentically claim as part of what it offers to the world? We think it is possible. Is it something that would put America in a strong competitive position in relation to others? We think it would.

We are not suggesting that justice for its own sake is simply rhetoric or a glossy public diplomacy and public relations campaign. There is a fundamental and concrete application of the idea that stares us in the face: food, water, and medicine. Even absent the 2008–2009 global economic downturn, a shocking proportion of the world's population does not have reliable access to one or more of these and has little expectation of better access in the future. The return of relative prosperity to the West will not by itself fill those gaps. It may make them worse.

Really striving to provide basic human needs on a consistent basis is one big way to pursue justice for its own sake. There is no possibility of human dignity in the absence of those basic needs, no opportunity to strive for other forms of justice when you've first got to conquer starvation and disease.

Let's render this in a very concrete example. What can and should America do next about global intellectual property regimes? If that sounds like an arcane issue miles away from social justice and of interest only to academics and to trade lawyers in Geneva, think again. How the world treats intellectual property is becoming, if it is not already, one of the most important determinants of the future distribution of justice (*as well as* wealth) on the planet. It is key to understanding and anticipating who owns, cares for, shares, and profits from human creativity. And when it comes to medicine it is the most important ingredient of the answer to the question of who can access pharmaceuticals, and thus who can cure disease and who cannot. What does a social justice leadership proposition need from intellectual property policy?

It needs first and foremost an explicit recognition that intellectual property regimes are issues of justice not simply economic efficiency. The arguments and disagreements about IP are not just business model problems for corporations but are foreign policy issues for countries. This is one of the most serious issues for both economic growth and justice, far beyond the short-term profits of music or pharmaceutical companies. Intellectual property law is about culture and cures for disease, and ultimately how to distribute and reward the knowledge that makes both possible.

Ask a citizen of South Africa to define a weapon of mass destruction. She is likely to answer "the cost of antiretroviral treatment for HIV/AIDS." Can you blame her, knowing that 100 million people may die in Africa from a disease that can now be treated as a chronic condition in the United States? In a recent AsiaBarometer survey that asked, "What are the most important things in life?" citizens of Korea, Japan, China, Hong Kong, Taiwan, Singapore, and Vietnam each responded very differently—with one remarkable exception. In each country, "being healthy" was ranked number one.[12]

The debate over pricing and availability of drugs in poor countries can feel sometimes like a passion play. It engages highly charged ideological conflicts about the deep morality of ownership and the value of life. The competitors, from Lou Dobbs to Médecins Sans Frontières to Universal Music to the Catholic Church to the U.S. Trade Representative's office and the National Institutes of Health, are swarming to define what this issue is really about. And they all have good arguments. It is in fact a set of arguments about property rights in the knowledge economy. And it is about the economics of how to create incentives for private-sector research and development. It is also about trade deficits, surpluses, and competitiveness, as well as safety, national security, government subsidies, and technological trajectories.

Perhaps foremost it is an issue of what constitutes a just society and what a presumptive leader will and will not do to promote justice. There is no reason for the United States to lag in a competition for that role. We do not need a newly populist-style fight on a global scale about how intellectual property enforcement exaggerates the concentration of both wealth and health among the already rich and healthy. Nevertheless, that is a possible conclusion, and never more so than in the wake of the 2008–2009 global financial crisis.

It is not an attractive, sustainable global leadership proposition to say the United States will win that fight. It would be a better leadership plan to say the United States will *transcend* that fight by recognizing and acting on the notion that to protect the most vulnerable is the sine qua non and true measure of a just society. When Americans give that goal pride of place—not only in the fights over pharmaceuticals but in parallel issues where we have both something to gain and something to lose—they tell the rest of the world what they stand for. That is the essence of a just society leadership proposition in the first part of the twenty-first century.

We think this can be very good news for the United States. There is no presumptive global leader better positioned to contribute to basic human needs around the globe than the United States. Put simply, Americans have the technology, the people, and the audacity of attitude it takes to make progress on these goals. They even have some money to spend if they decide it is a priority. It's a combination competitors can't match. The Chinese have the wealth and the people but not the technology. Global philanthropies and corporations have the wealth and the attitudes but not the people and the access needed to the range of technologies. Religions have the attitudes but not the right mix of wealth, people, and technology. There are other would-be competitors with parts of the package. If Americans don't step out ahead of them, others will make the best of what they have. Let's beat them to it.

4

PURSUING A TWENTY-FIRST-CENTURY WORLD ORDER

The basis of much of Western contemporary wisdom rests with older societies such as ancient Greece. Sometimes, however, that wisdom falls short in a changing world, and the present political global climate offers such an example. Earth is no more the center of the universe than the United States is the center of the twenty-first-century world order. America still has some gravitational pull, but other nations have slipped out of their orbits or found other orbits. The challenge of world order is how to keep the planets (international players) from crashing into each other or breaking the system apart.

Like those of Ptolemy, the works of Thucydides are another example of brilliant but now misleading ancient Greek wisdom. "The strong do what they have the power to do," he wrote of the claim made by the Athenians at the height of their power, "and the weak accept what they have to accept."[1] Much of history has validated this claim.

But it's significantly less true today. The power-influence gap, the difference between possessing power resources and converting them into sufficient influence to alter others' choices and shape outcomes, has been widening. That was a seminal lesson of the Bush years. It's equally apparent in the Obama years. Although less negativity toward the United States has meant less power-detracting effect, it has not had much of an influence-enhancing yield. And it's not just a U.S. problem: China has been getting more push-back from those around the world who are happy to do business and diplomacy together but not strictly on Chinese terms. The same dilemma will confront all who might aspire to great power. The possession of power is not the same as the exertion of influence. And it is certainly not the same as control.

So what will it mean to be a leader of world order in the twenty-first century? Here's one thing we are confident of: there won't be a single moment at which the next world order clicks into place. No comprehensive G-20, G-8, G-2, or G-something conference, no trumpets blaring, no treaty signing, no white smoke. But people will be choosing more boldly among competing propositions about how world politics ought to be ordered and conducted.

A competitive United States will need to get over the various versions of ideological convergence stories propagated over the last two or more decades. First there was the post–Cold War triumphalist end of history: capitalism and democracy for all. Then came the indispensable nation: nothing could be done without the United

States. Then the new Rome emerged: unipolarity. Then integrative international institutionalism: bring others in but keep the system largely as it has been since World War II. Is that the best we have to offer? World War II ended more than sixty years ago. That's roughly three generations past—even more distant from today than World War I was from the Civil War. How peculiar it is, then, for Americans, who see themselves as relentlessly forward-looking and oriented to better futures, to be so frequently stuck in a dated conversation about the unique advantages of the post–World War II international system.

It's not a matter of adjusting "pole-counting" to include the so-called rising and emerging powers. Nineteenth-century multipolarity is not making a comeback. Is it plausible to now imagine a small group of great powers dividing up the world—this colony for me and that one for you—and controlling the global economy in classic center-periphery terms? Could one group be writing the rules of cooperation and collusion that others would have little choice but to accept? Today's world encompasses not only those rising and emerging powers but many of the more than 190 nations finally emerging on the global stage after long histories of colonialism and superpower dominance. These nations are particularly assertive of their own interests and identities. With regionalism strengthening and deepening politically as well as economically, and cross-regional relations developing between regions that used to have little more than pro forma contact, a veritable alphabet soup of summits and associations—BRICs (Brazil, Russia, India, China),

IBSA (India, Brazil, South Africa), SCO (Shanghai Co-operation Organisation), EAS (East Asia Summit), UNASUR (Union of South American Nations), EU-LAC (European Union–Latin American and Caribbean Foundation)—has been emerging. A "World without the West" can be seen in some trade relations, security cooperation, and other patterns of exchange and interaction.[2] What makes these relationships distinctive is that they neither oppose nor accept Western rules—instead they seek to render Western rules less relevant by routing around them.

In this systemic context we believe that a new American leadership proposition for world order depends upon an actionable articulation of what we call *mutuality*. Mutuality is not self-denial, altruism, or the denial of nationalism. No nation can or will be for others instead of for itself, and national pride of place is an incredibly strong force in human consciousness. Americans still harp on their exceptionalism. China links its newfound formidable capacities to past imperial greatness. Russia fumes with wounded pride and flexes its revanchist muscles. But in a global age it is more essential than ever to have a credible claim to using one's power and position for seeking out actions and outcomes that serve shared interests, and using authority and power in the service of those actions and outcomes. That's the definition of mutuality.

It sounds simple, but it is not, because mutuality means sharing decision rights along with military, financial, and other burdens. Mutuality also points to a radical redefinition of what Americans have in mind when they use the term *multilateralism*—in particular, binding Americans to the same principles and rules that they ask others to observe, and redressing unbalanced bargains carried over from the Cold War era that strongly and unfairly favored the United States on issues as broad as nonproliferation and arms control, intellectual property and agricultural trade, and of course on the right to use military force.

Those principles of action might be perceived by some Americans as costly. What mutuality offers in return is a platform on which to build a world order leadership proposition that will advance three mutual goals: security, a healthy planet, and a healthfully heterogeneous global society. Security does not mean being the world's full-service security provider; it does mean being a security enhancer, and most especially not a security detractor. The goal of a healthy planet takes hold of the fact that environmental problems and movements are now fully global phenomena at the center of human lives, not abstractions about global public goods, externalities, and opportunity costs. Advancing a healthy planet means being a leader not a laggard in the pursuit of solutions. Acknowledging societal heterogeneity recognizes the potency of identity and takes hold of the great diversity of human experience to turn it into a virtue not a vice, a source of new and recombinant ideas, not fear and hatred.

No major global player has yet articulated a world order proposition around these ideas. That is a huge opportunity for American leadership.

Is World Order Oxymoronic?

A leadership proposition about world order needs to define its own terms and scope—not so much to satisfy academic critiques as to clarify to its audience what exactly is offered. Let's begin by specifying what *leadership* means when it comes to world order.

A leader is not a provider. Leadership starts with this foundational understanding: no single state and for that matter no international organization, economic system, religion, or any other actor or force can by itself define, determine, and provide world order on its own. Although it has become fashionable to state this as a new or at least newish reality, it has been true of world politics for a very long time. At any moment it was not true, we would be living under something that would be world government (whether it went by that name or not). We should not expect more from leaders than what they are by definition capable of providing.

What, then, is world order? American international relations theorists build their story about global politics on top of a simple proposition: the defining principle of world order is anarchy.[3] Anarchy means a lack of formal governance, a system in which there is no legitimate authority to make and enforce rules. Anarchy does not necessarily imply disorder, however. Anarchic systems can sometimes be highly ordered; it's just that the order won't come from an accepted and legitimate authority with enforcement power. It has to come from somewhere else, some other kind of process.

Historically order has come from three main sources: the power to impose and enforce; the authority to set rules and norms; and slack in the system to absorb costs and cushion shocks. This is the heart of today's world order problem: all three sources are in very short supply in the twenty-first century.

Most people today would agree to the notion that dignified and meaningful human lives rely on some level of world order. Most would prefer not too much government. Despite the still occasionally heard pleas for world government, there is a broad appreciation of some of the advantages of anarchy and, even more so, the disadvantages that would come if human beings actually did manage to stretch one single authority over such a large and heterogeneous species and planet. Freedom, experimentation, innovation, and diversity would suffer. Too little government, which is where it often seems like the world ends up, has other problems. We need to find a balance somewhere in between. That's one shared ingredient of what world order ought to be.

A second ingredient (not always shared) is that world order is not the same thing as peace. Of course more peace is better than less, all other things being equal. But all other things are not always equal. Of course it is better to bring about change without violence. But there are times and circumstances when people judge that to be impossible, and the wishful thinking that goes along with it wildly irresponsible. Most of us hate this fact, because (in sharp contrast to what was true for most of human history) there's very little romanticism around war left in our collective souls. The majority of people on this planet now see organized violence as "dead weight loss," wasted blood and treasure, the worst way possible to achieve a political goal no matter how valid or legitimate that goal may be. We never fully rule out war, however, because we know deeply that there are times when the only thing worse than war is peace with no change. E. H. Carr in *The Twenty Years Crisis* eloquently stated this profound fact of international politics: in the absence of settled political means for bringing about change there will sometimes be no alternative to war. No society on this planet has proven him wrong.

World order is definitely not the same thing as stability and status quo. It is often counterintuitive for Americans to acknowledge that proposition. During parts of the Cold War the overwhelming fear of nuclear conflict merged with the notion of stability simply because instability was just such a frightening prospect. Some will remember the "domino theory," "escalation ladders," and "mutually assured destruction." This evolved into what was then a positive and powerful statement about America's role in the world as preventer of nuclear war—and thus "stabilizer in chief."

It was always a second-best solution. When the fear of possibly unbounded consequences from instability (nuclear war) faded a bit into the background, terms like *stability* and *status quo* began to sound to others rather reactionary, particularly when they were being promoted by a country that gains the lion's share of benefits from unbalanced bargains and is able to shift the costs effectively onto others. Status quo is much less attractive when you have less, and especially when you feel you may be about to do better, be it in absolute or relative terms.

In short, a world order leadership proposition that generally privileges stability and status quo over innovation and experimentation is not viable, especially when there is less power to impose and enforce it on the one hand and more aspiration to alter it on the other. A leader that reduces risk for itself while depriving others of the opportunity to take risks that they want and sometimes believe they need to take is not going to be a leader for long. No single player in the international game gets to define for others what risks are worth taking—whether that be with regard to climate change, nuclear power, genetically modified crops, or anything else.

This leads to another statement of what Americans need to unlearn about our views of a world order leadership proposition. World order and *Pax Americana* are not the same thing. For those (and there are many around the world) who saw the Bush administration's theory and practice of American foreign policy as being a major cause of global *dis*-order, simply removing the Bush administration and reversing its disorder-generating practices is not the same as credibly offering real leadership for a new form of order.

As hackneyed as the phrase "new world order" sounds, it is something that much of the world actually needs, and knows that it needs. The catastrophic financial crash in autumn 2008 put the final nail in the perceptual coffin of the post–Cold War interregnum. The end of Wall

Street as we knew it—via the fall of Lehman Brothers and the humbling of Citigroup, Morgan Stanley, and Goldman Sachs—was the other bookend to the fall of the Berlin Wall. The old order, with the power to impose and enforce, is gone, and it is not coming back. A new world order means new principles of order that reflect both a different distribution of power in the world and a diversity of purposes. It does not mean the imposition of a new order through old principles of U.S. power and U.S. purpose.

One view is that with the corrosion of older forms of world order, military power (somewhat ironically) rises to the top as a principle and technology of order that governments will turn to. That's not an absurd proposition: for much of international political history, military power made the difference; it was the differentials in military power that defined the strong and the weak. It is still better to have more military power than it is to have less, but in today's world military superiority has not been the handmaiden of strategic success. In Iraq, the U.S. "shock and awe" campaign led to anything but "mission accomplished." In Afghanistan, the toppled Taliban has been resurgent and al-Qaeda has been displaced but not destroyed. In Somalia, Ethiopia readily removed the Islamist regime only to find its plans for quick withdrawal overtaken by renewed Islamist insurgency. Israel encountered roadblocks in Lebanon in 2006 and Gaza in 2008–2009.

To be sure, military power has substantial value for basic deterrence and defense. It retains value as a bankable asset but less so as a spendable one. Shrewd strategy can help: The Bush Iraq surge and Obama endgame may potentially avoid worst-case scenarios there, although it still would be hard to claim success in any net assessment given the costs and consequences along the way. The Afghanistan outcome in late 2010 (after more than eight years of warfare) still hangs in the balance. But amid the prevalence of asymmetric warfare, the politics of hearts and minds (a hackneyed phrase that is still on the mark), and various international and domestic constraints, we're not likely to see a change in the assessment made by Dennis Blair (then admiral and head of the Pacific Command and later director of National Intelligence), that "the use of large-scale military force in volatile regions of underdeveloped countries is difficult to do right, has major unintended consequences and rarely turns out to be quick, effective, controlled and short-lived."[4]

Two Positive Starting Points

The travails of American power over the last decade have demonstrated two very important and positive things about world order leadership—which we now have to learn deeply and internalize for the next decade. One is about the component characteristics of a leader. And the other is about the process of innovation, how new notions of leadership evolve into practical offers of leadership and come to replace those that are currently accepted. The dilution of military power as an ordering force does not leave a vacuum in its wake. On the contrary—it opens up space for other force components. The three components of a world order leadership proposition are now these: authority, effectiveness, and vision.

It's a pretty simple equation in the abstract. Authority is the *right* to act. Effectiveness is the *ability* to act. And vision is the *reason* to act. A plausible and attractive leadership proposition requires that all three components be in place and that they be reasonably consistent and compatible with each other. Consider what it feels like to others when there is a serious imbalance. Effectiveness without authority makes you a threat. Vision without effectiveness makes you an empty windbag. Authority without vision is bound to corrode over time—and more quickly in today's world.

To actually create and sustain authority, effectiveness, and vision in balance—in the eyes of potential adherents and followers—is the critical task of leadership. Each requires meaningful innovation from where we are today. So before we look more closely at what can make up authority, effectiveness, and vision for world order in the next decade, we have got to see more clearly what is distinctive about innovation in this domain, because Americans in particular have relied on some self-referential myths about innovation that serve them very badly.

The myth of innovation goes something like this. You have a product or a service that is meeting some important demands in the marketplace. It isn't perfect—nothing is. But it is getting incrementally better on one or another dimension that your most important customers tell you they really care about. Innovation happens, then, as the product improves gradually through what Clayton

Christensen calls "sustaining technologies." As he puts it, "what all sustaining technologies have in common is that they improve the performance of established products, along the dimensions of performance that mainstream customers in major markets have historically valued."[5] Christensen was talking about desktop computers, disk drives, off-road motorcycles, and other industrial products, but he might as well have been talking about world order, which you can usefully for the moment think of as a service (if not a product) offered by a leader to the market of potential followers.

Now imagine the United States as a leader and producer, and "mainstream customers in major markets" as America's most important allies and friends over the last sixty years. The United States has added a lot of what Christensen would call "sustaining technologies" over the years. Extended deterrence and its various operational adaptations were sustaining technologies that constituted an important innovation for NATO and other U.S. alliances both formal and informal. The North American Free Trade Agreement (NAFTA) was a sustaining technology for the postwar trade regime. Of course Washington has fallen behind the demand sometimes, but American strategists have then worked hard to catch up by listening intently to what their mainstream customers (most important allies) say they need. That is an important kind of innovation and it generates real improvements in U.S. world order leadership "service."

The problem is, it's not the only kind of innovation. And it's not actually the kind of innovation that matters most in critical times of change. Christensen's key insight is that disruptive technologies matter more. A disruptive technology is a different solution to a redefined problem, a way of serving demands that are deeply felt but not exactly what the mainstream customers say they want. It is disruptive technologies that almost always lead to the failure of leading firms and their replacement by new competitors.

What's critical and counterintuitive is this: a disruptive technology is not better on all dimensions than a sustaining technology. In fact, disruptive innovations generally are *worse* performers, at least in the short term. Disruptive innovations are therefore often not what mainstream customers say they want. Although they underperform on some dimensions at the moment they are introduced, however, disruptive technologies have a steeper trajectory of improvement and evolution. And some customers—usually not the mainstream customers that garner the most attention—can see that trajectory, and so they want to jump on it early because they believe that at some point the curves will cross and what was the disruptive innovation will become the leader. Christensen puts it like this: "disruptive technologies bring to market a very different value proposition than had previously been available. Generally, disruptive technologies underperform established products in mainstream markets. But they have other features that a few fringe (and generally new) customers value. Products based on disruptive technologies are typically cheaper, simpler, smaller, and frequently more convenient to use." Personal computers were the disruptive innovation that undermined main-frame computers. Transistors were the disruptive tech-nology that undermined vacuum tubes. Health mainte-nance organizations were the disruptive technology to conventional health insurance. In each case, the disrup-tive technology was cheaper to start but also less capable, less fully functional, less advanced in the eyes of the most sophisticated consumers. Today, the cheaper and less capable netbook is the disruptive threat to laptop com-puters.

In sum, at the beginning of a period of change, a dis-ruptive world order leadership proposition does not have to, and should not be expected to, exceed the perfor-mance of existing leadership models and propositions, and certainly not along all dimensions. In fact, a disrup-tive leadership proposition can be "worse" or less fully de-veloped on many dimensions and still disrupt the exist-ing order. It can do so particularly if it appeals to new and fringe followers that the existing order does not serve; even more so if it promises a steeper trajectory of im-provement. At some point in that trajectory, of course, the lines cross, and the adherents to the old (and now dis-rupted) technology trajectory will leap onto the other curve (or be left behind). That's a fundamental mecha-nism and trajectory of innovation.[6]

Think of how the disruptive innovation perspective sheds light on conventional American understandings of world order. How many times have you heard variations on this argument: alternative leadership propositions cannot compete with the American version because they do not have universal appeal or universal applicability. Here are some claims that should sound familiar: The "Chinese model" is not a viable option because one cannot imagine a world of state-capitalist, export-driven economies devoid of liberal political ideology. The "Singapore model" is not a viable option because only a small number of very small states can possibly achieve that kind of sophisticated entrepôt status. Radical Islam is not a viable option because of its nihilist elements and tendencies, and its foundational need to define itself in opposition to a vilified enemy. The "Japanese model" as it was talked about in the 1980s is too bound up in a specific culture. "Anti-Americanism" is not a real alternative because it offers no coherent end state other than the reduction of American power and presence. And so on.

Let's put aside for a moment the question of whether the American leadership proposition is really as universal as it purports to be, and focus instead on what the disruptive innovation dynamic teaches us about competitors. The whole point of the disruptive innovation argument is to show that a more limited leadership proposition, one that does not have the universal applicability that America's might have had, can in fact compete with, and even supplant, the existing order.

In fact, that's the way international political change generally comes about. The competitor doesn't have to do everything and offer everything that the incumbent did or does. It is a classic mistake to presume that because an alternative world order proposition doesn't perform all the functional tasks that a current one does (or promises), it is by definition not coherent and by implication cannot supplant existing arrangements.

This is a game of politics—which means it is not like the replacement of one scientific theory by another in a paradigm shift, in which the new theory has to explain everything that the old theory did plus some additional unexplained content. A disruptive leadership proposition only has to appeal on its own accord. In fact the challenger may benefit from offering a less capable, less fully functional, but also less burdensome and expensive "product" that appeals to a different audience for precisely those reasons. Notably, it will be seen by a significant subset of that audience, and eventually by adherents to the old order or old product, as having a steeper trajectory of evolution.

The question for the next decade is not whether the postwar American world order leadership proposition will be hit by disruptive innovations. It will. Indeed it has already. The real question is only *who* will disrupt. Either Americans disrupt themselves; or someone else will disrupt them.

Disruptive Innovation for World Order Leadership

What are the elements that coalesce to create disruptive innovation? Let's start with the first and irreducible ingredient of international politics: *power*. The purpose of power is to enforce and, at times, to impose. But enforce and impose what, exactly? Part of the reason that power seems to have lost some of its efficacy at present is because the endpoint of what power is trying to enforce and impose has changed. It has changed because the central security dynamic of international politics has itself shifted from the problem of dominance to the problem of systems disruption.

Dominance of one polity over another—whether historically it took the form of conquest, slavery, colonialism, occupation, or something else—is traditionally the central concern of international relations. There is a good reason for this: aspirations for and fear of dominance through interstate aggression have long been key elements of world politics. Some schools of thought say this is the natural and necessary condition of international relations.[7] Perhaps it will be the case again in the future, but for the moment that's just abstract theory.

In practice, today's major powers certainly have their differences, disagreements, and conflicts. But they are not seeking to establish traditional forms of dominance over each other. America and Russia may again slip toward a coldish stand-off on many fronts, but there's no return to Cold War–style confrontation in the offing. There are real conflicts of interest accompanying China's rise, but it is difficult to see how they lead even in the medium-term future to the traditional security challenges of dominance through violence among major powers. Iran's quest for nuclear weapons, whatever its precise motivations, is almost certainly not a stealth effort to support the invasion by Iranian armies of the territory of Iraq or Israel. Even the modern Middle East, rhetoric notwithstanding, is less a story about conquest than ever before.

The central security dynamic for most states outside of a few particularly backward regions is now the problem of *systems disruption.* World politics today depends upon an elaborate and interweaving lattice of complex systems through which the stuff of political economy flows: money through transnational markets, goods and hydrocarbons through sea lines of communication, people through airports, ideas and commerce through telecommunications networks. Disruption of those systems is the major security threat because it is the thing that places most at risk the safety and prosperity of states.

The 9-11 attacks aimed at symbolic targets to be sure; but they were first and foremost a move to disrupt systems not dominate territory. Pirates off the horn of Africa are systems disruptors. Attacks on oil installations in Saudi Arabia are systems disruption moves, as would be a coordinated sell-off of dollar assets among the central banks of China, Russia, Brazil, and India. Together their armies can do little to dominate the United States, but their central banks (unlikely as the scenario may seem) absolutely have the power to disrupt. Even the principal problem of weapons of mass destruction at present is more a systems disruption than a dominance threat. American military planners don't worry very much anymore about a massive surprise nuclear first strike (what used to be called "a bolt from the blue"); they worry a great deal about the impact a 10 kiloton device would have on global flows—even if it were not to explode but simply to be discovered in a container at the Port of Newark.

Systems disruption is such a potent threat in part because the systems on which the world depends are now so tightly stretched. The food price shock of 2007–2008 vividly illustrates this point. It took relatively little alteration in the dynamics of demand and supply to drive global food prices up massively, which in turn spurred export controls, food riots, and the threat of starvation among millions. The estimates of deaths from a virulent flu pandemic run similarly into the millions, and economic costs into the billions. Climate change of just a few degrees magnitude could be even more devastating.

Comparing whether these transnational threats of disruption are worse than classical state versus state dominance fights is less valuable than cultivating an understanding of the differences in the nature of security challenges they pose and what power can do to counter them. This is now the core issue for a claim of power effectiveness: a winning world order leadership proposition has to put forward plausible ways to counter and (even better) immunize against system disruption.

It's ironic, but that is a meaningfully higher bar for power than defense and deterrence against most state-to-state dominance threats. The reason it is higher is because systems disruption has all the characteristics of *offense-dominance,* a term that Robert Jervis and others used to illuminate a core paradox of nuclear deterrence.[8] Put simply, offense-dominance describes a technological military situation where it is much easier and cheaper to attack and destroy things than it is to defend them (the opposite situation, *defense-dominance,* is exemplified by the World War I story of trench warfare, where it was much easier to defend claimed territory than to attack and seize territory from others).

In offense-dominant environments, defenders face these kinds of difficult challenges: The enemy only needs to attack one or another weak target, whereas the defender needs to defend every single one of what could be nearly infinite potential targets. The enemy can spend a few hundred thousand dollars on offense and force the defender to spend many hundreds of billions to defend against the attack. The enemy can hold at risk systems that the defender depends upon, and to the extent they depend upon those same systems much less than the defender does and don't share much of the benefits those systems offer, the threat to disrupt the defender is in fact entirely credible. The defender's power to control can be rendered nearly irrelevant by the enemy's power to disrupt.

Thus the critical requirement for effective power in an offense-dominant world under threat of systems disruption is to be able to make the systems we and others depend upon more resistant and robust to conscious, directed disruption. And at the same time, as we discussed in the previous chapter, we must make those same systems robust as well to random, unintended, undirected disruption. That is the kind of disruption that emerges not because someone is trying to do something hurtful but simply because disruption emerges at the intersection of risks of interconnectedness that nobody really understands (or can foresee, at least until after the catastrophe happens).

The global financial crisis of 2008–2009 is clearly a

prime example. It could have been made much worse had a determined adversary with good access to financial networks and a few hundred million dollars, or perhaps less, been gutsy enough to try to take advantage of the system's vulnerability in the first few months of 2009, multiplying and magnifying the damage.

Power is but one element among several that coalesce to create disruptive innovation. *Authority* is the second—of course an inherently contentious notion with a diverse set of entailments in any political environment. It's probably most contentious in the international sphere. Who can and should be able to claim the right to act in the name of, or set the terms of action on behalf of others who are not part of a shared political community? Yet with all that, some concept of and debate about authority has always played a role in international politics.

A forward-looking world order leadership proposition needs a new (and probably disruptive) understanding of what authority is and what it can and cannot do. Such an understanding must come from a reanalysis of the relationship between authority and legitimacy. Authority is linked directly to legitimacy—and not legitimacy that is claimed by the putative source of the authority but legitimacy that is recognized by others. That has never been truer than in today's Copernican world, where it is less a question of whether one presumptive center of authority has sufficient and appropriate legitimacy, than it is a competition among several possible centers of authority for where legitimacy resides.

This guarantees a historically high degree of contestation. It is a contest in which the United States starts with a bit of a handicap and we need to be clear about why. The handicap is partly a problem that follows from the way in which Americans think about authority in world politics. U.S. scholarship in contemporary international relations takes the concept of anarchy, as we suggested earlier, a bit too seriously for its own good. Yes, the absence of a legitimate governing authority above and beyond the state is a good starting proposition for the development of academic theory and research programs. No, it is not such an outlandish assessment of what the real world is like that it shouldn't be used as a theoretical assumption regardless of how productive of research it can be.

But anarchy is also at the end of the day just a theoretical assumption, and it can get in the way of concrete reasoning about foreign policy behavior. Put simply, the academics' focus on anarchy has tended to make American scholarship and policy just a little too skeptical about the presence and importance of legitimacy, authority, and the intimate relationship between the two in international politics. There may indeed be no legitimate governing authority above and beyond the state in today's international system. But that is not the same thing as saying there is no legitimacy and no authority that matters. Because there clearly is a desire and a demand for both in today's world.

The handicap is also a legacy of history. When it comes to legitimacy and authority, it should be pretty clear now to dispassionate analysts that American policy makers made a cardinal strategic error in regard to the post–World War II order. It's the one thing that every presumptive leader is told never to do. They overpromised and underdelivered.

That is not to take anything away from the important successes of twentieth-century American-led world order. John Ikenberry is absolutely correct when he emphasizes this point: The liberal postwar order was a breakthrough in many respects and particularly of course in continental Europe.[9] Containment on balance did what it was supposed to do and eventually helped bring the Cold War to a (mostly) peaceful end. Cold War administrations "took their responsibilities for world leadership with a seriousness that . . . I found awe-inspiring," wrote Sir Michael Howard.[10] Decolonization in Africa and Asia was neither as violent nor as tumultuous as it might have been. And real effort was made at times to move the Middle East onto a trajectory of peaceful change. Given the plausible counterfactual histories of what might have been under different world order leadership stories, the real history does deserve enormous respect, and the United States should (and of course does) gain legitimacy for authority claims from it.

But Americans have gained quite a lot less ongoing legitimacy than they would like to believe. That's partly because the historical record is considerably more checkered than they like to admit. The pro-democracy claim for Cold War foreign policy was, for example, reasonably strong in Eastern Europe. Although power considerations did enter in, there was an undeniable authenticity to the gratitude expressed by the likes of Lech Walesa and Vaclav Havel after 1989. When it came to what Americans called the Third World, however, it was a very different story. Unless one accepted the "ABC" definition of democracy—"anything but communism"—it was hard to deny the immense gap between political rhetoric and policy reality. Iran, Chile, Somalia, Nicaragua, Honduras, and El Salvador are just some of the cases that we know about, and there are certainly others that the historical record (when and if it is declassified) will add to the list.

It may well be that, even so, American foreign policy has been more pro-democracy than any other major power. But this gap still made for greater *relative* hypocrisy for the United States than for others, who made no such or fewer claims to principles in the first place. America thus invited the world to hold it to a much higher standard, then at best met a moderately higher standard and in many cases not even that. Overpromise and underdeliver—a guaranteed way to corrode people's respect and trust.

And then there was the arrogant triumphalism of the 1990s. It has become a bit of an intellectual parlor game in American elite circles to criticize, even scoff at, then-popular ideas like "end of history," "indispensable nation," and "unipolarity." What Americans have not really done is to pay enough attention to the emotional and political impact these ideas had on the rest of the world, where America's presence is so keenly felt. Yes, much of this 1990s literature was heavily self-referential; devoid of any historical perspective or sense of irony; short-sighted in the extreme and willfully blind to how it would make non-Americans feel about their choices and place in the world.

But whereas Americans are relatively good at criticizing themselves and engaging in positive historical amnesia—leaving ideas like these behind as if they never really happened—the rest of the world doesn't do that so easily, nor can they afford to do so. Many other societies have longer time horizons than Americans do. Fundamentally, however, what Americans believe about the nature and meaning of their own presence in the world is still an important determinant of what international life is like for many other states and societies.

The Obama administration has masterfully changed the tone and tenor of this particular issue. Americans rightfully view the ability to do that as a triumph of the democratic process. But for people in other parts of the world who don't get to vote in American elections, such changes in American thinking and whatever actions result surely also have the tenor of arbitrary change, sometimes even capriciousness. For them, it is capriciousness that really matters.

The same was true of George W. Bush's "good versus evil" claim to authority. Washington's governing elite has left this meme behind and would probably prefer not to think about how deep it ran. Can the rest of the world afford to forget, or not keep in mind the possibility that the pendulum may swing rapidly back? Of course not. That, too, could be a triumph of the democratic process, if the American electorate realigned around a candidate in 2012 who was as different from Obama as Obama was from Bush. There is very little legitimacy to be gained in the eyes of others from that kind of oscillation.

The international institutions that were an important part of the American world order had their own over-promise and underdeliver pathology. Consider the original vision of the United Nations as proclaimed by one of its founders, Secretary of State Cordell Hull: "There would no longer be need for spheres of influence, for alliances, for balance of power, or any other special arrangements through which, in the unhappy past, nations strove to safeguard their security or promote their interests." These are honorable sentiments of the kind that state leaders love to insert in speeches but never realize in practice.

The 1948 Genocide Convention, one of the first major treaties of the new global body, made the "never again" pledge after the Nazi Holocaust, only to have the world witness "yet again . . . and again . . ." The Universal Declaration of Human Rights is often invoked but infrequently has any real impact. The international economic system, though avoiding the very worst protectionist mistakes of the past, has worked much more poorly over time and is now (at best) stuck. The Doha Round of trade negotiations was originally named (and sold to the world as) the "Doha Development Round"—a label that was conveniently dropped later on when it became clear that delivering on that promise would require some concrete, material, and costly compromises.

And when it comes to economic ideologies and reigning narratives about what it takes to create wealth, the financial crisis that started in 2007 has driven perhaps the most extreme oscillation. Overpromise and under-deliver could have been the crisis's mantra—from Eastern Europe to South America to Southeast Asia and beyond, the deregulated and investment bank–led capital lever-age system and globalized "flat world" that Americans sold turns out to have done little or nothing to create sustained value. The greatest irony of all? It was massive capital accumulation in a communist country where the state plays a very significant role that provided the under-lying juice, in the form of domestic (renminbi) savings re-cycled into dollars.

Americans can claim the legacy of late-twentieth-century international institutions as meaningfully a product of American leadership and emphasize the global public goods that these institutions provided. Or they can step back and say that the institutions took on lives of their own and that no one should blame America for their overpromise and underdeliver performance. What the United States can't do is have it both ways at once.

And now America has changed its story yet again, along several very critical dimensions. In the wake of the 2008–2009 financial meltdown, it was governments, not markets, that made the most important decisions about capital allocation in the global economy. In the U.S. case, the government did that with other peoples' money. After two decades of neglect, Americans are now suddenly tell-ing themselves and the rest of the world that wealth cre-ation lies in next-generation infrastructure, clean technology and energy, and responsible systems for health care provision. Why should anyone believe this? Why should anyone think that if the massive American bet on the role of the state in the economy turns out (or is perceived within American politics to turn out) a failure, the pendulum won't swing dramatically in the other direction, toward a neo-Reagan style Washington that rejects a state role in capital allocation even more fully and even more religiously than it did during the 1980s? What kind of legitimate authority can come of that?

Neither power nor authority alone can produce the necessary disruptive innovation for world order leadership. The third and final element is *resiliency*. If world order is a system, how resilient is that system within its environment to changes and shocks that are expected, unexpected, and sometimes even intentionally designed by others to undermine its stability? A leadership proposition about world order will not attract many followers if the order it proposes seems intensely flimsy or fragile. And that is another very high bar to reach in today's world.

There is a useful analogy to the problem of resiliency in cell biology. The challenge of maintaining order in a living system is called *homeostasis*. The single-cell organism is the simplest system of living order we can imagine. It has a huge homeostatic advantage, because it can take in across its membrane what it needs to maintain itself and excrete out across that same membrane all its garbage, waste, and poisons into the external environment. As long as there is a big external environment and not too many single-cell organisms in it, the organisms can function.

Multicellular organisms face a harder homeostatic challenge, because the external environment is farther away from any individual cell. These systems need to develop sophisticated mechanisms for allowing some things from the environment into the system, a way to detoxify wastes and move the poisons far away. As the organism gets larger and more complex, and as the population of organisms grows, homeostasis takes up a greater and greater proportion of biological energy. In fact the human body spends a surprising percentage of its energy doing exactly this.

And so it is with international political systems in the contemporary world. An advertisement about green environmental initiatives that Royal Dutch/Shell created in 2007 framed the argument appropriately for leaders: "Don't throw anything away. There is no away."

The world order challenge has changed in the same respect—more than anything else as a result of demography and technology. It wasn't so long ago that some nations could send their criminals to Australia; divide up a continent like Africa to act as a heat sink for European great power competition; or use strategies of colonialism to deal with falling rates of profit in the capitalist core (if you favor Marxist discourse). Others fought proxy wars in the Third World to take steam out of the Cold War pressure cooker in Europe. Even recently nations could "offshore" their pharmaceutical clinical trials to "underdeveloped" countries where a few "adverse events" or side-effects would be less visible. All these constituted a source of resiliency, the ability to insulate the core activities that made up the system from all the gritty stuff that went on somewhere else.

The space for throwing those gritty things "away" has shrunken drastically, however. The subset of what are commonly called "failed states" that are really weak but well-connected states are no longer "away" because they are not meaningfully insulated from global systems. Just the opposite is true, thus necessitating concern for them in a world order leadership proposition. The jurisdictionally ambiguous zones that make up much of the Internet, some free trade zones and trans-shipment arrangements, offshore banking institutions and pools of what are called "dark capital"; these represent similar challenges. They are not "away" from the system in any meaningful sense. What happens in those places are no longer negative externalities that somebody else can worry about at some unspecified future time. Any plausible world order leadership proposition needs to take account of these fundamental challenges to resiliency that are present and are not going away.

Who Are America's Competitors?

Can anyone compete with the American leadership proposition about world order? Of course they can—and do, on a regular basis now that the TINA mindset is mostly gone. Are those competitive leadership propositions fully articulated in terms that we understand, with a fleshed-out political philosophy that pretends to universality, a clear end-state logic, and a crisply specified role for every international actor like some modern-day Great Chain of Being? Of course not. But that's not the threshold that matters for disruptive innovation, and it is not the threshold that the rest of the world believes a competing leadership proposition has to meet.

The ongoing debate about the future of the dollar as global reserve currency shows what this looks like in practice. In 2009 a broad range of countries—China, of course, but also Russia, the United Arab Emirates, India, and others—expressed deep concern about the future value of their dollar holdings and the broader, negative consequences of continuing to rely on the dollar for such an outsized proportion of global reserves. Some concrete alternatives have been put forward, ranging from gradual diversification of national reserves to more elaborate proposals that would try to build global markets for an alternative, such as a basket of currencies along the lines of the International Monetary Fund's (IMF's) Special Drawing Rights (SDR).

Anyone can sympathize with the fear and frustration that the People's Bank of China must feel. If you were holding around a trillion dollars of U.S. Treasury paper and could only sit back and watch the U.S. government create new money at an unprecedented pace with a euphemism like "quantitative easing," you too would fret about inflation corroding the value of your reserves.[11] Nobody likes losing the kind of money that sovereign wealth fund investors from the Middle East and Asia lost when they rescued Wall Street money center banks in 2007 and 2008. If you had broader aspirations to match or exceed U.S. power and influence in other parts of the world, you might be frustrated as well with the constant passive gains and advantages the United States gathers from its de facto position of seignorage.

But sober global macro-economists remind us of the so-called facts: there is no fundamental competitor to the dollar, almost by definition. The euro is backed by an awkward confederation of national governments that have their own fiscal policies; the 2010 Greek crisis had to happen somewhere in the euro zone eventually; who knows how that plays out over time and the likely next time? The renminbi isn't anywhere close to full convertibility, and at the end of the day, do global investors really have long-term confidence in the stability of governance by the Chinese Communist Party? Buckets of currencies are still just buckets; the value of something like an SDR is ultimately just the agglomerated value of its ingredients. And when it comes to markets in which to hold reserves, there's nothing that comes close to the U.S. Treasury market in terms of sheer size, liquidity, price transparency, and so on. We're back to a kind of monetary TINA: whatever the frustrations and grumblings, there just is no plausible alternative to the dollar as global currency.

As a full replacement immediately, the dollar has no match. But disruptive innovation in world order leadership does not depend on an immediate, comprehensive replacement. The Chinese government can do the math;

it knows that to dump dollar assets boldly would canni-balize the value of their remaining reserves. They have no pressing need or desire to cut off their nose to spite their face (no matter how much it would also hurt the United States). That is why gradual, disruptive innovation is the way it goes: a swap account at the IMF for SDRs; the gradual development of markets for SDR-denominated bonds; a set of policies to promote the use of renminbi for bilateral trade settlements with particular countries; renminbi currency-swap agreements; and permission to Hong Kong banks to issue renminbi-denominated bonds. That is exactly what is happening in 2010. The next move will probably also be incremental.

There's an apocryphal story about a boiling frog that says if you throw a frog into a pot of boiling water, it will naturally jump out to save its life. But if you place the same frog in a pot and slowly turn up the temperature one degree at a time, the frog will never realize what is happening. We should not expect to wake up one day and find a full replacement for American-led order any more than the British woke up one day in the twentieth cen-tury to find their global position displaced by the United States. Instead an empire may find its leadership position corroded by partial, nascent, and sometimes less effective alternatives that—critically—attract the interest and com-mitment of others because they promise a steeper long-term trajectory of gains.

That is the logical progression of what we have written about elsewhere as "the World without the West," and it is the logic of a real competitor to the American world order leadership proposition.[12] Let's be clear: the Chinese example is not the only one out there, as we discussed earlier. But it's a good example because it illustrates the way in which challenges are likely to appear as unfamiliar configurations on the horizon, and how they tend to be discounted by American elites.

The discounting is not absurd on first glance. It is reasonable to doubt that (unlike previous historical power transitions) a rising great power would directly confront U.S. leadership—in a world stocked with nuclear weapons there is no intentional and rational way to get to what used to be called "hegemonic war."[13] But where it becomes absurd (and self-defeating) is to reason from that to the view that this means there is no way to challenge and compete with American leadership. This is to commit the cardinal sin of a declining power, which is to underestimate the creativity and strategic initiative present in others. What can be perfectly rational is for challengers to seek to route around American power (rather than confront it directly). The ultimate goal is not to win a conflict per se; it is to create a world in which American power is increasingly less relevant to what happens.

What is the world order proposition for "the world without the West"? It's built first and foremost around the concept of dealmaking between autonomous, hard-shelled states. In other words, state determination trumps self determination. Fuzzy notions like "global civil society" and -isms like "internationalism and liberalism" are put aside in favor of concrete statist decisions that meet each other openly at an unreconstructed bargaining table. States recognize no real rights or obligations other than to fulfill agreed contracts. And international institutions have no legitimate business other than to serve and facilitate these ends.

This world order proposition offers a transactional rather than a principled order, even in terms of rhetoric and atmospherics. (If there's a slogan or image to capture that feeling, it would be that the word *deal* is more important than the word *norm*.) It uses the technologies of connectivity, what Westerners call globalization, to create an order that reinforces its domestic governance principles (state power and prerogatives trump individual and societal power); and insulates its governments from pressure for political liberalization. It proposes to manage international politics through a neo-Westphalian synthesis comprised of states that bargain with each other about the terms of their external relationships but staunchly respect the rights of each to order its own society, politics, and culture without external interference. In other words, states should deal with each other over technical standards, trade arrangements, foreign exchange, and the like. They should not judge each others' electoral or legal systems, press freedoms, or cultural policies.

That many readers will see these notions of political order as reactionary, retrograde, and unsuitable for the modern world says more about the mindset of the West than it does about the magnetism of the ideas. Although we surely have moral and ethical sentiments about these issues, we are not making a moral judgment. What we think on that score doesn't matter for the argument. Neither should anyone reading this book stop at a moral judgment. Instead, first make an *empirical* judgment about whether this world order proposition is in fact present and gaining ground in global politics. If it is or might, any negative moral judgment you might make should simply add urgency to the task of generating a new American world order leadership proposition that can outcompete the ones you judge morally deficient. That's precisely what we believe is necessary and urgent.

What to Do Now

The most important new ingredient for a forward-looking American world order leadership proposition is this: A concept of *mutuality* that in practice demonstrates how the leader will use its authority and power for shared rather than selfish interests. It sounds obvious and straightforward, but it isn't so in practice. Here are some things with which mutuality can easily be confused.

Mutuality is not the denial of national interest (that would be as unrealistic as it is illegal for most states, including the United States). But leadership in world order will not be achieved if mutuality is left as an afterthought, a second-order effect of pursuing one's own national interest, especially in a world with an ever-increasing number of states that have the capacity to do so. That just isn't enough given the shift in the central security dynamic to system disruption. On the other side is the opportunity: To be the one casting the national interest in these more shared and balanced terms while others do not is a leadership play.

Mutuality is not altruism, which is the doing of things

for the benefit of someone else at a direct cost to one's self. Altruism is a precious human trait and it is not entirely absent from the world of international politics, regardless of what realist theories assert must be true by definition. Sometimes, for example, a humanitarian act is basically just a humanitarian act—in other words, pretty much what it seems and not a cynical cover for twenty-first-century economic imperialism or cultural penetration of a weakened society.

But altruism is not a meaningful principle of order because it simply is not sustainable across time and space. And it wouldn't be so even if there were not opportunists who look for ways to take advantage of altruistic impulses and behavior (in fact there are always some of these out there). Americans might very well celebrate acts of altruism on the international stage, and they might try to counter the almost inevitable reinterpretation of these acts as fundamentally self-serving (someone can always tell a story to make it sound that way, and someone usually will). But they had best not think to rely on the good will that occasional acts of altruism generate to sustain a world order leadership position for the United States.

Mutuality is not reciprocity, or at least not what is known in international relations theory as *specific reciprocity*.[14] Reciprocity is a principle of exchange relationships; specific reciprocity is an exchange relationship in which the accounts must balance out in the short term, at each specific act of exchange. It's "I give you a tariff reduction and you give me access to your banking sector" with the terms being "if and only if" as well as "I'll take my concession away if you take away yours."

Specific reciprocity is an important ingredient in the negotiator's toolbox. And it is conveniently easy to render in game-theoretic models. In fact, the core insight of Robert Axelrod's influential book *The Evolution of Cooperation* was precisely that a strategy of specific reciprocity—"Tit for Tat"—could outperform other strategies in iterated prisoner's dilemma games and lead to sustained cooperative outcomes under some interesting conditions.[15]

But cooperation under anarchy through specific reciprocity, as important if episodic as it can be in international politics, is also not a viable world order leadership proposition. In fact it is fundamentally about cooperation in the *absence* of leadership—a good thing perhaps, but not the same thing. And it is not so robust a finding as fans of *The Evolution of Cooperation* would like to imagine—change the underlying conditions of the game and what looks like a stable cooperative equilibrium can quickly and easily erode. Specific reciprocity is just not very resilient in an increasingly complex world.

What we mean by mutuality is somewhat closer to the related but distinct concept of *diffuse reciprocity*. Diffuse reciprocity retains some characteristics of an exchange relationship, but one with a more robust time and scope, in which accounts do not need to balance at every round of exchange but can do so across time and across issue areas. It might be best characterized by this statement: "I'll do this for you today with the expectation that sometime in the future you will do something for me that will roughly correspond in value and bring us into some kind of approximate balance."

A familiar principle in close personal relationships, it is

present, if not exactly common, in international politics as well. Reduce the importance of "exchange" per se in the equation, and you have something that is quite close to mutuality. Here's an articulation of mutuality that we think makes sense: "I will do this because we both benefit. Not in precisely equal measure necessarily, but not so unequal that either one of us is deeply disadvantaged. In the longer term, an ongoing set of mutuality moves will roughly balance out the accounts and leave us all better off than we were, and in a rough balance that we both can feel pretty good about."

A cottage industry of international relations theory spells out the impediments to building a system of interstate relations on this basis. Yes, mutuality requires a degree of trust or something like it that is often lacking. More important (and precisely), it requires some shared foundation of foresight about the future that is very hard to establish. Yes, it is vulnerable to domestic political dynamics, misunderstanding and misperception, and all the other dilemmas of relationships established without firm and well-defined contracts that can be readily enforced.[16]

But we are not talking about a complete system of international politics built on mutuality where interests can always be aligned—such a system is imaginary and it won't exist. We are talking about leadership, and particularly what a leader in the establishment of world order can do to cement that position. The most important thing is to maximize the application of mutuality where it does in fact make sense, and to do so boldly and visibly, exploring areas for mutuality that competitors for leadership are either afraid or incapable of exploring themselves. And for the United States there is in fact a great deal of space to explore.

Here's a prominent and timely example, one that manifests the goal of leadership toward a healthy planet laid out at the outset of this chapter: Carbon capture and sequestration (CCS) technology. Barring revolutionary breakthroughs in alternative energy sources over the next few years, the stark reality is that globally coal remains king. The world is going to continue to burn a great deal of coal for the foreseeable future. That includes the United States, India, and most notably of course the world's fastest growing consumer of energy and particularly coal-fired energy, China. Coal produces large amounts of carbon dioxide. CCS technologies don't magically make coal clean, but they do aim to capture the carbon and sequester it in some form so it does not reach the atmosphere (for example, by injecting it into underground rock formations).

CCS technologies are today extremely complicated, still rudimentary, experimental, and—not coincidentally—expensive. The investment in technology and resulting intellectual property behind CCS could be a massive source of profit for those who control the technology. Apart from the direct sale of CCS systems to users, a viable CCS system would dramatically enhance the value of every single coal mine and coal producer in the world, and that is an enormous and widely distributed set of players.

Climate change negotiations are, as everyone knows,

plagued by disagreements over who will bear the costs and who will reap the benefits. Developing countries are naturally concerned that America's rather dramatic conversion to green religion over the past few years, along with the massive private and government-subsidized investments in technology that this has brought, will restrict their own development. Developing countries worry that climate change treaties preaching global public good will lock them into paying royalties and licensing fees to Western holders of patented technologies that they will need to meet carbon reduction goals. They have reason to worry: The pharmaceutical industry and other intellectual property–intensive sectors have rarely taken an attitude of global public good toward their commercial prospects in developing countries, even when they begrudgingly acknowledge issues of life and death.

Why should anyone expect that the alternative energy technology sector will act differently? A CCS breakthrough in the United States would be a tremendous source of bargaining power on many dimensions—climate change, trade negotiations, and even security relationships in places like the Middle East and Eurasia. (If you can capture and sequester carbon from burning coal, then light sweet crude from Saudi Arabia and natural gas from Qatar and Russia are not so precious as they otherwise would be.) There would be enormous potential and surely temptation to leverage that technology as much as possible to enhance American power and influence in situations where we've been at something of a disadvantage.

That, however, is part of the prior century's world order leadership proposition. The right move for the future is to enact the principle of mutuality by giving away the CCS technology to the world. More precisely, perhaps the United States should license it along the lines of something like the General Public License used in some open-source software, where everyone can use the technology, and extend and improve it, subject strictly to the condition that any improvements and extensions must be given back to the community for the use of all.[17]

This would be a powerful example of acting in a way that serves global interests, using American technology for shared not selfish objectives. The leadership proposition does not lie in the abnegation of potential selfish benefits that one gives up, in theory, by licensing the technology royalty-free. It lies in the contribution to shared interests that one makes by distributing the technology widely and in such a way that the knowledge gained in practice from using it in diverse circumstances gets cycled back into the system for the benefit of all. And, of course, in the meaningful contribution to carbon reduction and climate change mitigation that would also benefit everyone.

World order leadership means, as we have said, redressing unbalanced bargains locked in from a previous era. Mutuality is a useful way to begin to ask how some of these bargains can be rethought. The CCS example can be extended to other intellectual property–intensive sectors such as pharmaceuticals and agricultural genetics.

The same principle of mutuality can be directed toward other visibly unbalanced bargains. The Doha Round and agricultural trade are one example. Responsibility for the deadlock on this issue is shared widely—not only Americans but also Europeans, Japanese, Brazilians, Indians, and others have unbalanced bargains to protect. Those bargains have been in place for a long time, long enough that their perverse effects are almost by now a background assumption. But the harsh reality of agricultural subsidies is profound: When an American cotton farmer floods global markets because he is guaranteed a price more than twice as high as the world price, with the difference made up in subsidies (subsidies that help push his income over $1 million), the Mali farmer who supports a family of twelve on less than $2,000 each year has his income pushed lower. Meanwhile the American taxpayer ends up paying double. They pay over $4 billion per year (itself more than the GDP of some African countries) for the subsidies at home, then they pay foreign aid abroad (for example, $40 million to Mali, tellingly symmetrical to the $30 million its state cotton company lost to falling world cotton prices). These are only the direct, first-order negative costs. To resolve this issue would resolve both a domestic and an international problem, bringing benefits abroad and benefits at home, a domestic solvency gain from rebalancing for greater global mutuality. That may just be worth taking on the wrath of domestic constituencies.

Opportunities to rebalance bargains around security are actually quite easy to find. It is neither possible nor necessary for the United States to be as much of a global provider of security as it was during the Cold War. To be a security enhancer (as well as to avoid being a security de-tractor) is a chance to reconfigure the bargains with our European allies, with Japan, with South Korea, and with friendly regimes in the Middle East. That's more than asking others to share the financial and human burdens of providing security, it is also offering to share authority for decisions that impact their interests as much or more than ours.

Mutuality, in a radical redefinition of what Americans often mean when they use the term *multilateralism,* means adhering to the same principles and rules that Americans ask others to observe. That too may sound obvious and straightforward. But the United States has not generally observed this commonsense notion in practice.

The days of "feel-good" multilateralism, when a global leader convenes a conference or a meeting of a global in-stitution to legitimate what is essentially a unilateral de-cision, needs to be boldly left behind. Telling other coun-tries that they should own the burdens of multilateral policies but not own the decision rights that define those policies is over. That might have been a plausible articula-tion of power, but it was never one of multilateralism, at least not multilateralism that matters to anyone else in the world.

"Tough-love" multilateralism is a better way to think about it; in which the tough love applies both to other players and to ourselves.[18] Let's remember that multilat-eralism is just a process, not an outcome in and of itself. Genocide prevention is an obvious example of a valuable outcome for multilateral institutions to pursue. But although process matters, it's not nearly enough by itself to define a world order. Tough-love leaders focus on getting things done and use the process to leverage greater effectiveness. If multilateral institutions cannot act to prevent overt genocide, a presumptive leader will not hide behind any particular process. That may mean a thinner layer of international governance in some respects. But it will also be a more sustainable and meaningful one.

Beyond the particulars of policy and process, a believable story about world order needs an embedding vision that inspires and embraces a vast diversity of human beings. The United States has offered such a vision before. Its future global leadership depends on doing so again. In a world in which identity is such a powerful force—with localized and particularistic identities of nationality, ethnicity, religion, and race so intense and so often divisive—America needs to positively affirm global societal heterogeneity along with equivalent respect to our own domestic heterogeneity. That's not always an easy extension to make, but it's a possible one.

Nothing about mutuality says that countries cannot or will not bargain for unilateral advantage in world order games. Of course they can and will. What it says is that to be a leader is to identify and press the places of mutual advantage to the maximum extent possible. That's not a prerogative of leadership; it's a *prerequisite* for world order leadership in the twenty-first century.

Doing this is not just a matter of tweaking public diplomacy, reviving what are now clichés about American exceptionalism, or resorting to TINA, even implicitly. It requires credibly conveying a commitment to mutuality as the guiding approach to world order and demonstrating the capacity for effectiveness in getting done what needs to get done. That's what it takes to be a leader of a twenty-first-century world order.

5

BEING STRATEGIC ABOUT THE FUTURE

Imagine you are watching a news broadcast in 2020. The New Eurasia Research Consortium reports on the results of its instant global public opinion poll. This morning they asked 100 million people around the globe a simple question: "What is your opinion of the United States today?" Eighteen percent say they hold a favorable opinion of the United States. Sixteen percent see the United States in a negative light. Sixty-six percent—a full two-thirds of those polled—responded "don't know" or "no opinion."

Surprising? Probably. Inconceivable? We don't think so. A bad scenario for the world? In many respects, yes—but much of the world might not see it that way. Bad for the United States? Definitely.

Over the course of the second half of the twentieth century, what the United States did and was about to do occupied a special place, and usually first place, in the thoughts of most globally minded people. But such a preoccupation is not a law of nature. Mindsets change quickly when the reality of influence is altered. Americans would almost certainly be the last to realize that their impact on the rest of the world is a fraction of what it used to be, for better or for worse.

How else might this loss of influence manifest? Here are some other imaginary stories that might appear on that same news program. Today officials confirmed the long-rumored relocation of World Bank headquarters from Washington to Brussels, following the IMF's move to Singapore the previous year. U.S. equity markets today for the first time fell below 30 percent of global market capitalization. The Shanghai-Moscow-Mumbai maglev train made its first run last week and this morning set a world speed record for land transit. The best-selling book in the United States this year is titled *America's Lost Decade*. Sovereign wealth funds in the Gulf are looking to the United States as an investment opportunity of high potential: with a weak currency, a cheap but reasonably educated work force, and slack environmental standards, it's a great place to think about locating low-cost manufacturing for export. What is amazing to foreigners is how much time and energy Americans still spend on the blame game and finger pointing when it's absolutely clear to everyone else that nostalgia won't create jobs or much of anything else valuable.

The centrality of the United States to the international political and economic universe was overdetermined for much of the twentieth century. Its position rested on a heady mix of power, ideas, behavior, culture, physical and emotional reach, and more. When one or two of these ingredients underwent a bit of a cyclical downturn, the others usually ramped up to make up the loss. That's why the label "the indispensable nation" essentially rang true in its time. People around the world who heard that statement reacted positively or negatively depending on whether they thought it was a good or a bad thing for the rest of the world. But very few people said it was downright wrong.

Those days are certainly coming to an end. America's global challenge for the next decade is how to establish leadership for a different world. Forgive us for repeating it one more time: this is not simply a matter of undoing the damage incurred by the Bush administration. There's a deeper problem to solve and a more profound set of understandings to engage. We have put forward an argument in the service of defining and promoting a new American leadership proposition, one to which we think much of the world will be receptive. We have done so unapologetically. We are confident that if the United States gets it right, not only Americans but most of the world will benefit. This chapter lays out some of the hard choices that Americans will need to confront along the way.

First, one final twentieth-century anachronism must be left behind. Although there is nothing so beguiling for a state as a sense of invincibility, it's when you lose it that statecraft and strategy really get interesting. Few states have the luxury of experiencing anything like invincibility. Realist theories of international relations have long explained why. Since there is no international political mechanism to enforce agreements and contracts, the use of force as a means for settling disputes always lurks in the background. States are not constantly at war with each other or even preparing for it. But the looming recognition that there is nothing to prevent the use of force constantly conditions and influences what states do.

At the end of the day, security for states in international politics is scarce, expensive, and elusive, though not always, and not for all states. The United States has been particularly lucky in this regard. We have had considerable periods of history when threats to our security were distant and abstract rather than immediate and severe. For much of the Cold War the biggest threat, existential and extraordinary in magnitude, was also clearly understood and de facto deterred by a nuclear force that hid invisibly within concrete silos and under deep oceans. And then came the 1990s (ironically, an unfortunate period) and the post–Cold War world with its unipolar moment, its sole superpower. For more than a decade the United States reveled in a seductive sense of near invincibility. We fought ground wars against the world's fourth largest army in Iraq, halfway around the planet, and defeated it with less than 300 American deaths. We fought air wars without any American casualties (in Bosnia). Nobody could threaten us in a meaningful way. Nobody could seriously challenge our primacy. And it seemed as if nobody could do anything significant in world politics without our assistance—or at a minimum, our assent.

When others believe they can't defeat you in conflict or harm your vital interests no matter what, you are essentially secure—even in an anarchic world. This period has come to an end. That was inevitable. The question now is not so much how Americans, caught up in the expected partisan bickering of domestic politics, interpret and will interpret the meaning of their experiences in Iraq and Afghanistan. The more immediate question is how *other* global players interpret it. Here are a few notable data points: Russia felt empowered to directly confront the United States over missile defense. Iran has taken a more aggressive stance toward nuclear proliferation. Venezuela seizes every possible opportunity to provoke Washington and is actively organizing mini "antihegemonic" coalitions wherever it can. China for the first time in August 2007 publicly and explicitly noted that its enormous foreign exchange reserves empower the People's Bank of China to respond to unwelcome pressure from Washington to revalue the renminbi with sales of dollar assets that would cause significant dollar devaluation and a jump in long-term U.S. interest rates. And so on.

This is all to be expected because it is a return to normal international politics. When great powers lose the aura of invincibility (as all do later or usually sooner), others begin to probe for weak spots that were previously submerged. They start to experiment with opportunistic behaviors that they would have earlier eschewed. None of this necessarily means the end of extraordinary U.S. influence. Opportunistic probing for weakness and experimenting with new alliance possibilities does not mean that China or Venezuela or Russia or some combination intend to directly confront the United States for global leadership. (It *could* mean that; the point is that we don't need to lock in agreement on that issue for our purposes here.)

It certainly means that the United States will be facing new challenges—on many fronts and from many directions—and a gut-wrenching process of adjustment, both practical and emotional, to this new reality. It's not a new story: The United States of course went through a variant of this process after Vietnam, as did Great Britain after its imperial decline, Russia after the fall of the Soviet Union, and Israel since the 1973 Yom Kippur War.

How does the great power respond? They may not be logically comprehensive, but recent experiences suggest three general options. The first is to push back against the trend and try to re-establish the perception of invincibility. The Israeli argument about recreating "general deterrence" is a version of this approach. Ronald Reagan's first-term foreign policy—in particular, the massive strategic modernization program for nuclear weapons—had a similar motivation. Second, the superpower could negotiate deals now, to co-opt the rising challengers by offering them a greater stake in the status quo, thus preserving it. They would then lock in as much of the power balance favoring the superpower as possible. This of course was a central part of the Nixon-Kissinger "grand design" for detente.

Finally, the superpower could instead become a first-class strategic actor, using its still extraordinary power position in a much more calculated way. The purpose of such a move would be to maximize ongoing leverage over the preferences and decisions of others. The superpower would best do this in a way that emphasized its continuity of purpose and relative strength. Such a great power would neither aim toward re-establishing invincibility nor locking in the status quo. In such a way it would demonstrate not absolute strength, but strength. We believe this third response to be the only viable option for America in the next decade. What this means—as we have been arguing through the course of this book—is that Americans need to get much more serious about competitive strategy. To put it bluntly: When you're not invincible, you've got to be strategic.

How to Be Strategic

What does it mean to act strategically in world politics? A common and simple definition is something like this: Strategy is a coherent story about the world and what you want to achieve in it. This definition is often put forward by foreign policy makers. It is often used by corporate executives. And it is implicit in the somewhat extravagant term *grand strategy* that some foreign policy academics bandy about.

We believe it is a dysfunctional definition, particularly for a country like the United States. Strategy, we propose, should be a compelling story about making choices.[1] To be strategic is to prioritize, to leave some attractive opportunities on the table in the knowledge that you can't do everything. It means making difficult decisions when you hold strong conflicting values and can't maximize them at once. Anybody can tell a story about the world they want to live in. Strategy is the discipline of choosing the most important aspects of that world and leaving other stuff behind.

The goal of strategy is not to avoid or seek out risk, but to make intelligent decisions about risk. This definition of strategy has the crucial advantage of pushing to the foreground the necessity of allocating and focusing efforts. It also recognizes the central importance of another reality: That the other players in the game are smart and capable as well—perhaps not as smart or as capable, or perhaps more so. The other players make their own choices and prioritize against their own perspectives on the trade-offs they face. Critically, they may not see the trade-offs in the same way that Americans do.

To act strategically means having not only a coherent theory of the state of the world but an insightful view of how other players theorize about the state of the world, particularly when they do so differently.

Strategy and uncertainty are two sides of a coin. At the limit strategy is not about what you know. That's called tactics and execution—doing cleanly and efficiently what it is that you know how to do and doing it better every time. Strategy is about adapting in the face of what you *don't* know and what you *don't* control and learning as you go. Such learning must encompass the uncertainties in the world and the perspectives of other players on those uncertainties. And so the forward-looking question for foreign policy becomes this: How do great leaders develop adaptive strategies to cope with complex combinations of uncertainty, knowing and taking account of the fact that other leaders are trying to do the same thing?

The United States has not been as good at these ingredients of strategy as it could be. In part because of a historically lucky draw on geography and resource endowments, Americans have not always had to face the hard choices as directly and explicitly as many other states. That mindset has been bolstered by a culture that celebrates, sometimes excessively, the conviction that courage is defined as a dogged unwillingness to accept the necessity of compromise among objectives and values.

This is not an indictment of America; far from it. It's simply an honest recognition of that very messy place where psychology, culture, and politics meet. It is stressful for any individual to face a situation in which you have to choose among multiple values, all of which you hold dear. Big organizations like bureaucracies, corporations, and states tend to reinforce a natural individual tendency to try to reduce that stress. And the more power you have, the more deeply embedded this reaction becomes. If we are that powerful, maybe we don't really have to face the hard choices, but can instead force them onto someone else. In American culture, saying otherwise often paints you with the label of "timid."

The decisiveness that results from power is one of America's greatest cultural strengths. But like most strengths, when carried too far it becomes a weakness. And we believe that in the realm of the global competition of ideas it has in fact been carried too far. In a complex and rapidly changing environment it does not work well to repeatedly reinforce who we are and what we stand for. We know those things, and we know how they shape what we do, how we act, how we respond. Strategy is ultimately about how we influence what *others* do. And the most effective way to influence others is to focus deeply on their interests, their desires, and their needs—and then use our power, our beliefs, our commitments to direct our actions toward those things.

It is axiomatic, in our view, that better U.S. foreign policy strategies cannot be premised on the presumption that other global players will (or should) hold a similar set of understandings about priorities and trade-offs in world politics. They often will not do so, and for their own (sometimes very good) reasons. We believe it is just as important to develop effective and sustainable strategies for initiating international cooperation. These depend as much on shared understandings about the nature of those differences as they do on tight compatibility of interests among a very diverse set of players (which will be rare).

But before the United States is really positioned to take serious steps toward understanding how others view key trade-offs, Americans need to acknowledge their own. They need to look a few gut-wrenching choices straight in the face. And they need to articulate, for themselves and to those they wish to influence, a set of principles for deciding how to prioritize and choose.

To start down that road, we offer up four hard choices

that we believe will confront American foreign policy makers in the next half decade. These are not simply immediate policy choices, such as whether or not to declare a date certain for withdrawal from Iraq or an ultimatum for Iran. They are medium-term choices, issues that will define in profound ways the strategic environment for ourselves and others over the next several years. Each certainly has immediate policy choices connected to it. But it would short-circuit the purpose of this effort to reduce the importance of these issues only to those immediate policy choices. Profound value trade-offs go deeper than that, and each policy choice shapes our own and (just as important) others' expectations about how the medium-term future will unfold.

We present each issue within a story—some real, some imaginary—that represents the underlying value trade-off. After analyzing each, we close with a proposal for a candidate set of principles, or at least a coherent perspective, for how to face some of the most difficult decisions, communicate our goals and objectives to others, and use both to become more like world-class strategists in international politics.

Hard Choice #1: Statecraft in a World of Nonstate Actors

Consider what the following list of anecdotes suggests about the nature of power and influence in world politics. Al-Qaeda provoked the sole superpower into at least one and possibly several interstate wars. NGO-supported and -facilitated "color revolutions" toppled regimes in

Ukraine, Georgia, and the Balkans. IBM has recast itself as a "globally integrated enterprise" rather than an American one, despite its heritage as an American icon and its Armonk, New York headquarters. YouTube has, or will soon have, greater global influence over narratives about many international events than any government information source could dream of. Halliburton has opened its new headquarters in Dubai, where the CEO now lives and works. The Gates Foundation in practice if not in name runs public health policy for several African states. Private military contractors fought much of the Iraq War, after the initial invasion. Gazprom has been granted license by the Russian government to form its own armed security forces to safeguard pipelines, which pass across thousands of miles of Russian territory and hundreds of cities. These are concrete examples of the diffusion of power to nonstate actors in the contemporary world. So what? What, if anything, should America do about this trend other than note it?

A (weak) consensus view among American opinion leaders seems to hold that the overall diffusion trend will continue, with minor changes in the roles and locations of important organizations and individuals. Radical groups that span boundaries between political parties, social movements, transnational criminal networks, and governments—such as Hezbollah and Hamas—will remain ideologically problematic, but of minor practical significance—policy irritants rather than significant threats. "Super-empowered individuals" that act on a global stage, major corporations, and NGOs will still disproportionately have their main offices in the United States, and their activities will impact marginally, and mostly for the better, on America's power and reputation. The net effect of these actors on global problems will be mildly positive and generally consistent with U.S. policy goals in global health, security, and economic arenas. In other words, nonstate actors are mostly good news for American foreign policy, if much news at all.

Many elite policy communities outside the United States don't really share these views. There is an overall sense that confidence in state capacity is eroding in parts of the world more broadly and quickly than Americans recognize. It is expected that international NGOs, foundations, private firms, and perhaps even superempowered individuals will seek to almost fully take over key government functions in failing states. It is also recognized that these groups and individuals will increasingly come from outside the United States—not only Bill Gates and CARE, but also Richard Branson and Médecins Sans Frontières. There is a much deeper and more unsettling expectation, as we suggested earlier, that highly influential nonstate actors are about to emerge rapidly and visibly from the developing world: perhaps Lakshmi Mittal, a Hutchison Whampoa, or Dubai International Capital Foundation.

There is outside the United States quite a lot of ambition and also anxiety about these developments. Some fear that the rise of nonstate actors could further undermine operational sovereignty norms for states in what is already a very confused situation. There are deep concerns about accountability: To whom do these nonstate actors ultimately answer? There is fear of overly concentrated influence, analogous to what Americans would think of in market settings as an antitrust dilemma. In other words, charismatic super-rich individuals or foundations with extraordinary wealth, aggressively entrepreneurial leadership, a for-profit mindset, and strong ties to business may find themselves in (or even seek to engineer) situations that in the nonphilanthropic world would be seen as unacceptable concentrations of power. An extreme imagine-if: Would the Gates Foundation one day offer malaria vaccines preferentially to those countries that make the greatest effort to protect against piracy of Windows software? To even suggest such a thing sounds absurd, insulting, bizarre, illegal, and inconceivable to many Americans; but this kind of leverage is a real concern to many communities outside the United States.

American foreign policy makers need to formulate a clear and coherent point of view on the question of whether these diffusion trends are good news or bad news for the United States. It's no longer interesting to simply acknowledge that nonstate actors are important and deserve attention.[2] The question now is, what do we want to do with and about that fact? Is the diffusion of power to nonstate actors a trend we wish to accelerate, impede, ignore, or shape in some specific directions? U.S. foreign policy strategists need a clear perspective on the question of how policy can shape the growth and influence of nonstate actors to the benefit of U.S. global goals.

Al-Qaeda is the easy case; we know what needs to be

done with nonstate actors bent on violent extremism. It's the others that are more complicated. In practice NGOs have been largely synergistic with core American foreign policy goals. They have taken on programs that official foreign aid budgets unloaded. They have brought problem-solving expertise to bear that complements and often exceeds that within government. They have made significant contributions to economic development, state building, and civil society empowerment. And whereas NGOs have their own concerns about not being seen as too closely linked to the U.S. government, even at a distance "brand America" benefits often carry over to U.S. foreign policy. This strategic functionality, though, does not necessarily project forward. Two uncertainties that pose difficult choices are embedded here:

Widening the universe of nonstate actors. The Copernican world effect is imminent for NGOs. Brazil's Viva Rio tellingly describes itself as having been founded with a focus on local issues but "due to the multiple nature of security matters, Viva Rio has become more international."[3] BRAC (Building Resources Across Communities), based in Bangladesh, is the largest NGO in the global South, employing over 100,000 people, mostly women, and reaching more than 110 million people across Asia and Africa. Should American foundations now be in the business of consulting on strategy and implementation with rising NGOs that will be based in China and active in Africa?

Many other states are becoming positioned to reap the

gains of prestige and influence to which NGOs based in the West have become accustomed. Indeed powerful NGOs bring prestige not only for their state of origin but also for the people and society, building reputations for innovative capabilities and, possibly, shared values. A global competition in NGO action is coming. This can contribute to the principles of mutuality underpinning world order if the competition gets set up correctly. If it doesn't, the competition risks becoming a zero-sum geopolitical game.

From supplemental to central. Separate from and parallel to the question of the national origin of nonstate actors, what should be America's view when NGOs in the aggregate move beyond supplemental to much more central roles in governance? Consider the following scenario we and our colleagues have worked with:

> The world of 2015 is seeing new and dramatic forms of political reorganization. Technology and culture together enable the deconcentration and decentralization of power, simultaneously breaking down conceptions of the international community and weakening traditional international organizations, and undermining and replacing the functions of national governments with new experiments at the national, regional and local levels. States in some parts of the world are increasingly unable to provide basic governance functions to their

populations and so they withdraw, de facto "outsourcing" these functions to a variety of other actors, including private sector security organizations, humanitarian and health NGOs, and mega-philanthropists with global agendas.[4]

Is such a scenario good news or bad news from the U.S. perspective; a trend to be enabled or applauded or something to be combated? You don't have to go all the way to the "end of nation-states" stories to confront the hard choices: Who gets credit? Who has authority and responsibility? Who shapes and reins in the NGOs? And what is left that states are uniquely competent to do? We've already suggested an imaginary scenario involving public health and the Gates Foundation. To put an even sharper point on it, what if in the not-too-distant future a collection of extremely rich individuals from around the globe raises and deploys a privately financed military force as a peace operation, citing the unwillingness of the international community to stop ongoing genocide in Nigeria. Given the failures of the state system to deal with genocide, why not try a strategy that routes around it? That question is utterly apparent in many parts of the world and among many individuals and organizations that have little to lose by experimentation.

This takes us back to the underlying question: what role for nonstate actors in the global "division of labor" would the United States like to see? Here are two possible answers. The United States could try to deploy the power of nonstate actors based in America to position itself as a

determined ideological combatant in an increasingly po-
larized ideological world. That's not an "imagine if"—it is
what Andrew Natsios, former head of USAID, explicitly
suggested in the immediate post 9-11 environment. He
told some of his largest grantees and contracting NGOs
that they were now effectively instruments of U.S. policy
in the war on terror.

Or the United States could try to use its influence over
nonstate actors to position itself as a postideological,
technocratic problem solver providing basic human
needs like clean water and vaccinations in a world that is
tiring of everybody else's ideological battles.

It probably can't do both. And that raises quite practical questions of policy. Americans know that conducive
tax and regulatory policies have been key to NGO growth
and philanthropic giving. The United States spends a lot
of time and money on training sessions, consulting,
and other efforts to facilitate other states developing
their own more NGO-conducive policies. Washington often makes it a priority to engage NGOs in other states.
Should the United States keep doing that? In particular,
should the U.S. taxpayer subsidize it? Which solution do
we choose: the functionality logic of providing world order and moving toward just societies, or the geopolitical
competitiveness of "my NGO versus yours"?

Which institutions are more effective: NGOs or formal state-based international institutions? The nature
of American participation in international institutions
deeply affects the opportunities for nonstate actors. For
example, the United States may prefer to have the World

Health Organization (WHO) leading public health campaigns in Africa rather than Médecins Sans Frontières or the Gates Foundation, since the U.S. government's still-prominent role in the United Nations provides some influence over WHO's priorities and methods. U.S. policies can directly influence the appeal held by outside actors for important constituencies: For example, targeted foreign aid could just as easily mitigate the need for social services provision by international NGOs as by local radical groups—if we wanted to limit NGOs' bases for support among vulnerable populations. Alternatively, the United States could pull away from existing international institutions, free itself from what some see as dated rules of multilateral decision making, and pursue a set of much more decentralized extragovernmental strategies by engaging with nonstate partners to the exclusion of the World Bank and the UN.

One thing seems certain: American capability to shape the global rules of the game for nonstate actors will probably never be stronger than it is at this moment. It will almost certainly be weaker in the future. Since this is the U.S. moment of influence, what should be done about it?

Hard Choice #2: Unilateralist Caveat, Multilateralist Glibness

The problems with the Bush administration's penchant for the formulation of "unilateralism when possible and multilateralism when necessary" are well known. It got caught in the Thucydides fallacy we introduced in Chapter 4, of the strong not being strong enough to do what they want to do and the weak not being so weak as to always have to accept what supposedly they have to accept. The Clinton administration had a different formulation: "multilateralism when possible and unilateralism when necessary." The Obama administration's starting point here is much like Clinton's. But although we have learned to strike a better balance, we are still sidestepping the really hard choices.

Unilateralism is not a dirty word. The "when necessary" caveat for acting unilaterally is in many respects understandable. States still are an organizing unit of the international system; self-defense is a core right; and presidents have the constitutional responsibility to defend the nation and its people. The issue is *in extremis* or an elastic clause: Is the U.S. intent to resort to unilateral action only in genuinely extreme circumstances, or is a claim still being made for discretionary flexibility? For many around the world, and not just inveterate anti-Americans, the historical record and beliefs about deep-rooted American political culture cause doubts to persist regardless of who occupies the White House.

Unilateralism, to many Americans, suggests that the United States can and should drive the course of important things in world politics simply by deciding what U.S. actions will be. Phrased that way, the default position of U.S. policy becomes simple. "What we must do is make up our minds and demonstrate the will to execute. End of story." It's an attractive notion for an action-oriented culture that thrives on getting things done. And people in other parts of the world know what that means.

Americans have got to come to terms with their own and others' cognitive and emotional loading of the term unilateralism and they have got to do it now. Unilateralism means too many things: strong to some, short-sighted or stubborn to others. It conveys determination and purpose to many, and a failure to understand the complexities of the world to many more. These disparate connotations also cut their own ways as strategy. On the one hand, to convey determination and purpose can strengthen deterrence when it raises the possibility that the United States may choose to act if another actor violates important interests or even threatens them. But this uncertainty can also offer incentives to challengers—to gain the advantage of moving first (the "sucker-punch" approach), provoking U.S. unilateral action that others calculate will backfire.

It is hard to square the unilateralist caveat with mutuality. When interests are shared, unilateralism won't be necessary. When unilateralism is said to be necessary, it is hard to stanch the "me too" cascading effect of other states making their own when-necessary claims for acting unilaterally. Some of this no doubt is rhetorical sparring, convenient equating, for their own preference for unilateralism elasticity. But in some cases U.S. precedents likely tip the balance for states genuinely wrestling with their own tough decisions. The irony: This may be a more frequent and notable effect under the Obama administration than under the Bush administration since unilateralism would likely be interpreted as "even him," not just "of course him."

To counter unilateralist attitudes by simply evoking multilateralism merely sidesteps the hard choice, however. Multilateralism has become just as loaded a term. It sounds less resolute, less effective, less favorable to the United States. In the minds of some, it connotes a reasonable willingness to work with other global players according to at least a partial set of rules of the road. The deeper problem is that it is just too glib. The cons of unilateralism do not neatly translate into pros for multilateralism. If there was any doubt about the messiness and dysfunctionalities of multilateralism before the Copenhagen Climate Conference in 2009, there should be little doubt now. Beyond Copenhagen, consider Darfur, global poverty alleviation, or nonproliferation. There is more on the positive side of multilateral action than neoconservatives and other ardent opponents acknowledge, but there are also many more and deeply inherent problems than many academic international institutionalists or political Wilsonian internationalists claim. Those who set "the rules for the world," as Michael Barnett and Martha Finnemore perceptively show, often fall into their own organizational pathologies of global bureaucratization.[5]

Whatever the particular formulation of the multilateralism problem—collective action, free riding, tragedy of the commons, organizational pathologies—two dynamics hold. First, commonality of interests does not automatically lead to commonality of action. We have all heard these claims again and again: Everyone has an interest in avoiding nuclear war. Everyone has an interest in averting climate catastrophe. Everyone has an interest in pandemic prevention. But the extent of common action does not measure up to the scope of the problems.

Second, interests are not as common as people often want to believe. Many so-called global public goods actually are divisible and excludable, which is to say that they are not as public or global as one might think. Some lose more than others from climate change. It's an ugly but unavoidable truth—the Maldive Islands may end up below sea level while the Isle of Skye becomes a beach resort easily accessible by package tour. In a more profound sense, it's an equally unavoidable truth that some societies are better situated to compensate (with wealth, technology, or other sources of strength) when the shared costs of climate change appear.

The standard debate over whether unilateralism or multilateralism are good or bad general principles for U.S. foreign policy misses this crucial point. As we said earlier, the game of international politics is always a bargaining game. Unilateral action never determines a long-term outcome; it is just a single move in an iterated process in which other players get to make the next move. And multilateral action does not imply that we view other players' preferences and aspirations as being more important, or even as important, as our own.

The real underlying issue concerns the relationship between leadership and bargaining positions. It is about deciding what kind of global leader the United States wants to be in the next decade, and having just as clear a view of what kind of leader other players in world politics will accept as legitimate. Because that is a critical part of what differentiates a bargain from coercion. The rest of the world is at this moment powerfully ambivalent about the notion of U.S. leadership, no matter what. And it is particularly ambivalent about U.S. leadership in what are presented as ongoing bargaining games.

The nostalgia that some Americans express for the post–World War II period of U.S. global leadership, whether justified or not, is much less compelling for generations now assuming power outside the United States. Weariness and wariness around arguments that smack of American exceptionalism as a claim for leadership are widespread. The notion that U.S. economic and political systems and practices can and should be exported to the rest of the world is seen at best as naive, at worst as absurd and even noxious.

And consider this point too: the trend is running against American influence. It is part of a longer-term development that reflects the rise of alternative sources of power and leadership, and rapid technological change. These have created more distributed capabilities throughout the world. Around the globe beliefs have shifted from TINA (there is no alternative) to THEMBA (there must be an alternative). Quite simply, a significant percentage and possibly even a majority of people living on this planet today do not right now see U.S. power as a positive force in their lives. Whether they are right or wrong about that does not matter; it is what they believe and it is what they will act upon.

At the same time, there is a widespread and deep respect for distinctively American capabilities and achievements in innovation, entrepreneurship, higher education, and many areas of science. In some places, our relative success in the assimilation of diverse identities is admired. These are huge leadership assets that we bring to any bargaining table. But when it comes to joint endeavors to get traction against today's most pressing global problems—including nuclear proliferation, climate change, genocide, and responsible management of the international economy—these assets are not yielding sufficient payoff for American leadership in the global competition for claims to mutuality and a just society.

On many issues, the center of global political gravity has shifted from "America must lead" to "America must participate." There is a less prevalent but significant and growing perspective that sees even U.S. participation as no longer absolutely necessary. There are global players, individually and in groups, who are increasingly ready, willing, and able to route around the United States and attack global issues without U.S. contributions if the United States stands aside.

Let's pose again the simplest strategic question: Is this a good or bad thing for the United States? Let's not forget that generations of Americans have struggled with the perceived responsibilities of supposedly having to police the world. Leadership can sound more attractive in theory than it sometimes is in practice. It carries with it the patina of great influence, but it can reduce in important ways freedom of action, ability to take risks and experiment, and opportunity to free-ride on the efforts of others.

The single most important decision Americans need to make about leadership is this: To what extent, and with what instruments, can and should the United States encourage greater burden sharing, and even alternative centers of control, in the provision of global public goods? We need precise and clear answers to this question before we start obsessing about multilateralism, unilateralism, ad hoc coalitions, and other questions of institutional shape and process. If there is a trade-off between control and capacity, where does the United States stand?

A market metaphor about demand and supply helps clarify what is at stake. The demand for global governance created by the increased interconnectedness of globalization in all its aspects—economic, public health, communications, security, environment, and so much else—is not being met with a sufficient supply. The demand curve continues to slope upward, the only variable being how steeply. This means the supply curve has to run faster if it is not to fall further behind. That's the source of urgency. But even when the United States has been willing to sacrifice elements of control for the sake of capacity, it has tended to send "mixed messages," as Edward Luck puts it, of guarding against others encroaching on its prerogatives.[6] Go forth and solve the world's problems, embody the global will, but only as far and in ways that America determines. That didn't work well in the past, and it works even less well now as the demand curve slopes upward. It's not just that others' voices and votes need to be represented. It's that Americans need to become comfortable with real shared authorship, both voice in decision-making and pride of place in actions taken.

Elites outside the United States recognize that the United States does provide a disproportionate share of some critical global public goods, particularly when it comes to security. Some quite explicitly state their intention to free-ride on that situation for as long as possible. Of course, the United States stands to lose over time if rising powers are allowed to endlessly free-ride. But if the United States were to bargain seriously for greater contributions from others, Washington would almost certainly have to share decision-making power as part of the trade.

In concrete terms this dilemma will emerge most immediately and poignantly with regard to China. A China that contributes as a responsible stakeholder to global public goods will surely want to be more than a silent partner or junior associate when it comes to decision making. That very issue emerged visibly in 2009 around the G-20 and the IMF. It won't be confined for long. Along with the responsibility to make greater contributions, a stakeholder gains the right to have a greater say in the rules of the game regardless of the area of concern or extant institutional structure. If burden sharing also means the sharing of decision rights, is the United States ready to take "yes" for an answer? Most important, are we ready to take a "yes" from Beijing? How we handle that hard choice will be closely examined by just about every other powerful player on the global stage in the next decade.

Hard Choice #3: "Freedom and Democracy" in a Statist and Populist Environment

Imagine that it is 2016. A significant group of fast-growing, strategically important developing countries—for example, Indonesia, Nigeria, Venezuela, India, Iran, and Colombia—have clustered around an alternative pole of influence in the international system. This group has its own joint financing facility funded by People's Bank of China reserves. It has its own multilateral development agency, supported by Persian Gulf and Russian sovereign wealth funds. It has its own security organization, constructed around a successor to the Association of Southeast Asian Nations (ASEAN) Regional Forum, which pledges noninterference in the domestic security affairs of members coupled with absolute shared defense of external borders. And it is about to declare its own multilateral "Nuclear Systems Management Agreement" that is much more heavily weighted than was the Nuclear Non-Proliferation Treaty toward the expansion of cheap and carbon-free nuclear power as an energy source.

The governing principle for this alternative pole and its constituent institutions is state determination and hard sovereignty, rather than self-determination and individual political rights. Governments in this pole respect, to a fault, the sovereign rights of state determination. They bargain with each other over technical standards, trade arrangements, and currency alignments but don't touch subjects like electoral systems, cultural policies, legal systems, or press freedoms. They do not get distracted or distract others with abstract notions of individual autonomy, dignity, or sustainability. They create wealth and raise the standard of living their populations enjoy. They choose among variations on the theme of state-controlled capitalism. The target is economic growth that supplants rather than stimulates demand for political opening. "To get rich is glorious," as Deng Xiaoping said, and in this part of the world it has become equally a means of individual fulfillment and self-expression more satisfying and fulfilling than anything that democracy can offer. "One man, one vote" has become "one man, one cell phone."

Forget liberalism, universal human values, the "moral reliability of democracy," and other abstractions from Western voices. In 2016 there's no need to fight with these leftover twentieth-century ideas. For many in this new pole those ideas are just a mildly pathetic attempt by a declining hegemon to redefine as global and universal what is distinctly the product of a particular culture and a particular time that has now passed. These ideas can for the most part simply be ignored. The explicit contract between government and governed in this alternative world is an austere but workable populism: The role of the state is to provide economic growth and improved material welfare for the population, redistributed as necessary to sustain a politically mobilizing but not explosive and thus moldable tension between the "people" and the "elite."

American foreign policy makers need to be realistic about the plausibility of this kind of scenario. Most important, they need a clear-headed assessment of the key uncertainty surrounding its significance. The central question is, would an "-ism" like this succeed, or must it certainly fail, in a policy-relevant time frame?

There is a consensus view among the U.S. foreign policy elite, and it is close to this: Certainly there are "-isms" of this sort out there at present (as well as others), but each is fundamentally flawed in its own way, and none is as sustainable, durable, resilient, legitimate, or desirable as liberal democracy. Next, these alternative "-isms" may be short-term irritants to U.S. global goals. But they irritate mainly because of the *policies* that emanate from particular states, rather than because the alternative "-isms" themselves are of any real significance. Finally, if we deal with these states correctly today—limiting our downside exposure to troubling policies as they arise, while gradually working to expose the deeper flaws in their governing "-isms"—none pose a meaningful challenge either to core U.S. objectives or to the spread of liberal democracy. And so, for U.S. policy makers, the scenario is not just an extreme version of a real possibility, it's really just not possible. Is that view robust enough to build strategy upon?

Elites in many other parts of the world see this kind of scenario as possessing a much greater degree of plausibility. They do not view alternative principles for ordering of society and economy as simply romantic meanderings from a single "true" path of development. They do not dismiss these alternatives as quixotic efforts by semicharismatic individuals to define something different for the sake of being different. Whether they like it or not is a separate issue. There is a strong belief in the resilience of this kind of alternative "-ism," a readiness to see its fundamental sources of strength, to see that it has some advantages when compared to democratic liberalism—and most important, that it is in many ways attractive to vast populations in the non-Western, developing world.

This is not a matter of normative political philosophy. It is rather just a question of practical politics. If the governed populations see these alternative systems as legitimate, philosophical arguments about their long-term sustainability become nearly irrelevant.

Here are some discomforting truths of today's world. An alternative governance message that emphasizes order and progress (regardless of other ideological content) over democracy, one that places economic growth and poverty reduction before political liberties, is deeply attractive to a significant proportion of the global population. In the final analysis the global population does not see itself as having benefited meaningfully from an era of American-led globalization. Those winners outside the West who have in some degree benefited largely attribute their good fortune not to liberal internationalism or American ideals, but rather to state-directed capitalism run by illiberal governments.

This alternative "-ism" surely has its own tensions and problems. Taking on Google may not work as part of an information control and censorship strategy for China. Communications technologies and social media may yet contribute demonstrably to regime change in Iran.

Leaders in these and other countries dismiss such dynamics at their own peril. But we should not make the opposite mistake of forgetting that the core bargain and alternative balance constraining individual freedom and unfettered markets in pursuit of state order and shared societal progress has a very large natural constituency.

No charismatic leader has yet emerged to powerfully articulate the message of this "-ism" in a compelling way. There is no Lenin, no Jefferson, no Martin Luther King, Jr. of this world—not yet. Indeed, the clumsiness of someone like Hugo Chávez makes it seem as if the emergence of such a leader were impossible. But it is not impossible. Can we imagine a young, technologically savvy, educated, rich, non-Western leader combining elements of Lee Kwan Yew, Vladimir Putin, Nelson Mandela, Carlos Slim, and Muhammad Yunis? Do we know what we would say to that person, or—more important—to the over 4 billion people who might be listening to her?

This challenge sets up several hard choices. The first is how to recalibrate what long has been a systematic and ideologically charged claim on the part of the United States to have a massive say in the domestic political arrangements of other states. During the G. W. Bush administration this was both celebrated as democracy promotion and tainted by military intervention and selective application. But the internal contradictions of priority and purpose were hardly unique to the Bush administration. To be sure, there have been those such as Vaclav Havel who testify to America providing crucial support and inspiration for him and his country "to enter . . . into an era in which all of us, large and small, former slaves and former masters, will be able to create what your great President Lincoln called 'the family of man.'" But there also have been others like Emilio Aguinaldo, leader of what he thought was to be Filipino independence in the War of 1898. Instead that war ended in American colonialism. Aguinaldo raged that he had not "made war on the Spaniards for their [United States'] benefit, but for the purpose of our own liberty and independence."[7] Woodrow Wilson sought to make the world safe for democracy on the one hand but found himself serially intervening in Latin America on the other. These tensions are deeply rooted in American political culture, going back to the iconic conception of "a city upon a hill," unique and exceptional in our essence and the global role that flowed from that. For all the contemporary evocations, neoconservative and liberal alike, it was really an eighteenth-century poem by David Humphreys, a protégé of George Washington, that best captured the mantra:

> All former empires rose, the work of guilt,
> On conquest, blood or usurpation built;
> But we, taught wisdom by their woes and crimes,
> Fraught with their lore, and born to better times;
> Our constitutions form'd on freedom's base,
> Which all the blessings of all lands embrace;
> Embrace humanity's extended cause,
> A world of our empire, for a world of our laws.[8]

What the Obama administration says and does about democracy promotion over the next several years will be a very important signal to the rest of the world about what that deep conviction inside America really means for those on the outside.

The tension between democracy and interventionism is embedded in a deeper and yet more difficult question. What is the American view of the uncertainties surrounding the short-term impact and longer-term sustainability of alternative "-isms"? What is the U.S. strategy for managing that uncertainty? To put it simply, the U.S. government needs a set of conscious choices that is considerably more nuanced than the contemporary mindset of "engage versus contain," used, for example, in thinking about the contemporary rise of China. To continue the China example in an oversimplified but illustrative way: If we believe that China's system is likely to succeed in the policy-relevant time frame, we could attempt to accommodate it by building bridges to it, or even going so far as to become more like it. (If this sounds outlandish, think back to the debate about Japan in the 1980s.) Alternatively, we could seek more aggressively to undermine it by enhancing the ideological pull of democratic liberalism or by using realpolitik instruments to increase the perceived costs of the Chinese system. By contrast, if we believe that China's system will fail in the policy-relevant time frame, we could essentially ignore it—and allow it to run its course. Alternatively, we could try to accelerate its decline by forcing China to overstretch itself, for example by pressing Beijing to take more of a global leadership role on core issues such as poverty reduction and the environment, or by instigating a democratization movement in China. We could directly fight it by attempting to peel off important countries attracted to its system. These approaches obviously have different risk-return profiles. The point is that not choosing among them, or ignoring the fact that we might have de facto made a choice, is not a responsible strategic option.

There is a third difficult choice here, one that may not bear on immediate policy choices but will be profoundly consequential for how we view American domestic politics and how others view our presence in the world. The choice is about how global developments will impact our perspectives on populism. Leave aside the negative connotations that sometimes attach to the word. Populism, at its heart, is a belief that society (whether global or domestic) is deeply split between "the people" and "the elite"—two groups with internally shared interests that are necessarily at odds with each other. Baldly put, the people want redistribution of wealth and the elites want to bolster their relative position, and the most important social and political fights erupt where those preferences intersect.

The difficult choice is this: What do we say to populist leaders? The "freedom and democracy" trope doesn't effectively counter populist beliefs. In practice, democracy too easily becomes a tool of manipulation in the hands of populists. If you start from strongly populist presumptions, freedom and democracy will land you in a bad place. Populism suggests a pitched battle between opposed sets of interests. So if the elites win, you get exploitation. If the people win, you get majoritarian illiberalism. Not a good outcome in either direction.

The U.S. perspective on populism is mildly comforting in this regard: when the people win, populism is more bravura than delivering on policy. It's too blatantly redistributive and ultimately runs up against the fact that those from whom it would redistribute have sufficient power to check and resist. And thus it either fails economically, probably in a maelstrom of inflation and disinvestment, or it becomes politically repressive. Chávez can run a bombastic scam for a while, but not long enough to really matter.

Maybe so, and maybe not, especially when populism is fueled by expensive fossil fuels and other scarce resources that the rest of the world needs. Regardless, it can be a very long road to re-equilibration out of populist collapse. Societies get torn up in the interim. If all we have to say to populist leaders is "it won't work," we've not got enough to say.

So what is, from the American perspective, a signal of gross inequality that actually requires government action to redress, whether at home or abroad? In 2006 the CEO of Goldman Sachs earned more than 56 million dollars. Is that acceptable? The 2008–2009 financial crisis only put off the reckoning while making the underlying stakes more intense. If Wall Street bankers had the system wired for "heads we win, tails you lose" before the financial crisis hit, they certainly have used the "too big to fail" argument to their advantage during this crisis and further socialized the downside risk while keeping almost all the upside prospects for their private gain. Michael Lewis gets it right when he says that the lesson was not about a mistake in allowing Lehman Brothers to fail but in allowing a system that facilitated gargantuan success for itself and its Wall Street brethren.[9] In 2010 seven of the world's leading hedge fund managers took home ten-figure paychecks. It would be optimistic bordering on self-delusional for Americans to think that we are immune from a populist backlash in the next few years, regardless of the justification for and sensibility of policies enacted during a moment of crisis to stop what might have been a global economic free fall.

The challenge for Americans is to decide what to say both at home and abroad about economic redistribution. As we've argued a number of times in this book, in today's technologically enabled global competition of ideas, a powerful nation cannot endorse and enact one philosophy of governance at home, propose a different one for other countries, and even a third one for the international system.

Hard Choice #4: The Shadow of the Future

Are human beings ruining the planet for future generations? As critical and timely as this question seems, it is actually just part of a much bigger and more complicated leadership dilemma, which is this: What are human beings willing and able to do in the realm of *prevention?* Does the United States have what it takes to make prevention of future problems and crises part of a leadership proposition, with all the trade-offs and hard choices entailed in doing so credibly not just rhetorically?

In an old television commercial encouraging regular oil

changes, an auto mechanic stands with an oil filter in his hand and a seized-up engine on a chain above his shoulder. "Pay me now, $19.99," he says, "or (looking up at the engine) pay me later."

The oil filter metaphor bears on lots of gut-wrenching issues. How many of them is the United States able or willing to address?

- To engage in preventive diplomacy (or more?) when there are early warnings of genocide and other mass atrocities rather than waiting until they explode;
- To create standing global public health capacity on the front lines of where pandemics most likely break out rather than scrambling to keep up once infected travelers show up at airports;
- To correct fiscal imbalances before they crash an economy;
- To seriously address climate change and other global environmental issues before they pass beyond the points of criticality.

All of these are about acknowledging the shadow of the future, acting as if our children and our children's children genuinely matter.

All have to overcome the rationality of not doing so. It is a rationality of the moment that sometimes leads to irrationality down the road. It requires making cost-incurring commitments and trade-offs today for a benefit tomorrow. The future benefit may be greater than the present cost, but it is generally much more uncertain—and it is in the future.

The logic and politics of preventive action depend upon what economists call the "discount rate." Far from an example of arcane jargon, the discount rate is the critical variable in any argument about how investment should be made to prevent *some* bad things that might happen in the future. That's the really hard leadership challenge: Since there are an unlimited number of bad things that could happen in the future and limited resources today for prevention, what risks do we act on and when? How do we convince others that our choices make sense so that they wish to and will act with us?

The field of economics views discounting in a very clear way: Since an action today has a stream of consequences that emerge over the course of time, the future is typically discounted relative to the present when we think about costs and benefits. Why? Because as we move forward in time from the present, the cone of uncertainty widens—we might never have to pay the future costs. Something else might happen to wipe them away. Or if we suspect we will be stronger, richer, and more powerful in the future than we are today, then pushing costs out to the future makes sense since we will have more resources to deal with them then. And so on.

Politicians and public officials naturally have their own versions of discount rates. From a purely political standpoint the most urgent (and often dysfunctional) discount factor is about costs in this electoral cycle, not benefits possibly borne in some other one. Telling constituents that you spent their money today to prevent something bad in the future that might—or might not—happen is not generally a great campaign argument. People don't usually vote on the basis of counterfactuals. And as a policy matter there's always the full inbox of immediate stuff that demands attention. "I know I should get to that longer-term issue," a politician thinks, "but I'm swamped with matters close at hand."

Although that's a cynical view of politics, it is not an unrealistic or unfamiliar one. It's also a view we know is not a strong basis for strategic leadership. The future is generally closer than people think. The slack in the systems we depend upon is less, as we discuss in Chapter 4. We're running out of places to dump the externalities while we buy time to figure out how to clean them up.

Yet the appropriate discount rate is not a brute fact given to anyone by ethics or standard formulas that can be derived from economic or any other kind of abstract theory. And it matters enormously. Because the discount accumulates like compound interest over time, a small difference in today's discount rate can justify a substantial difference in policy and thus in outcomes ten years out. Minuscule differences in discount rates within a society or between societies, or for the globe as a whole, drive very large differences in how many generations for whom we end up acting as stewards.

In fact there is no general solution to the problem of knowing what anyone's discount rates should be. What we do know is that the two extremes make no sense. An infinite discount rate says that the future matters not at all, in which case we would invest nothing but simply consume everything we could at the moment we could. Only under the direst circumstances and for very short periods of time do humans live this way. A discount rate that is effectively zero means we are willing to impose no costs at all on the future for what we do today. This may appear at times ethically defensible—as in "do no harm"—but it doesn't make sense when you look more closely. Was it really our ethical responsibility to sustain the Anopheles mosquito for future generations, rather than build the Panama Canal? No one knows the future uses to which today's natural resources might one day be put. We cannot be certain that if we were to destroy the last samples of smallpox virus, we wouldn't have cheated a scientist in 2020 out of genetic raw material for a breakthrough discovery. We don't know that by eradicating smallpox in the wild we haven't opened an ecological niche that will be occupied by a deadly pathogen that is today unknown. It is equally true that no one knows what technologies could emerge to help future generations substitute for things that we may have deprived them of.

A strategic view incorporates the notion that we ought to think about making foreign policy "as if our children mattered." But without a clear view on what discount rates are and should be, "caring about the future" and "as if our children mattered" are slogans and nothing more. These give no guidance about how to make the hard choices that policy makers need to make. We can't prevent every possible ill that the future may bring, so which do we emphasize and which do we ignore? Most important, how do we convince others that they should make compatible choices?

Let's consider the environmental story. In the twentieth century—the so-called American century—Earth's population quadrupled. During the same period, industrial output increased by a factor of forty. Energy use increased by a factor of sixteen. Fish harvesting increased by a factor of thirty-five. And sulfur dioxide emissions increased by a factor of ten.

That is actually an extraordinary record of efficiency as well as wealth creation. Just four times as many people, enjoying forty times the industrial output, with only sixteen times as much energy needed to produce it. If we could rewind the tape of history and replay the last several centuries without the Industrial Revolution, would it be beneficial to have had tighter environmental restrictions? The air would be cleaner; the oceans less acidic; Earth probably a degree or two cooler; the range of species on the planet wider. But we would also be strikingly less wealthy. And we might have fought more not fewer wars with each other. The Industrial Revolution brought about vast capital accumulation—human, physical, and technical—and vastly increased knowledge stores and flows. These things created opportunities for future generations that would not have been available otherwise.

It is not just right-wing rantings or denials of climate science to pose this perspective. The counterfactual might be better than reality, or it might not be. That is a judgment we can't usefully make about the past. But we absolutely need to make these kinds of judgments about the future and we absolutely need to make them in conjunction with many other countries, cultures, and societies.

If Earth had unlimited resources and unlimited capacity to absorb carbon and other waste streams from these systems, we'd be cheering ourselves forward along the twentieth-century trajectory and celebrating the decreasing energy intensity of production as if it were humankind's greatest achievement. But it doesn't. And American political culture has been more resistant than most to the global environment narrative that has followed that recognition. Improbably, it was Al Gore's film about climate change, *An Inconvenient Truth*, that became the touchstone of broad change in U.S. attitudes. Talk radio hosts still argue about the science of climate change, but many Americans are swapping out incandescent light bulbs for compact fluorescents and recycling plastic bags (if they even dare to use one). Risk capital is getting serious about non–fossil fuel energy. In many respects Americans are catching up to a mindset that many others on the planet, particularly but not exclusively in Northern Europe, have held for some time.

A late start notwithstanding, Americans' financial and technology assets combined with dogged determination to fix huge and intractable problems like climate change position them well for a global leadership role on this issue if they choose to take it. But leadership takes more than this. The 2009 Copenhagen Climate Conference was a powerful demonstration of that fact. The United States came to this meeting with a very different policy position but without the ability to convince others that a newfound view of the risks and discount rates was the proper one on which to build concerted global action.

Shifting incentives for other nations depends on precisely what it is that Americans are doing, and not doing, as a result of their newfound orthodoxy. It depends also on what they tell, suggest, pay, cajole, and most important persuade others to do and not do, and how their orthodoxy and rhetoric interact with other global negatives they might wish to prevent.

This is a critical call for a vital kind of leadership. A successful international leader will need three skills. First, the leader will need to deeply understand the concept of discounting and be able to explain and justify it to both domestic and global constituencies. Most challenging will be to find common ground with states and societies that feel insecure, committed to and dependent upon very short-term growth prospects, and lacking in the stable institutional infrastructures that tend to lengthen the shadow of the future and thus modify discount rates. Discount rates can probably be changed through persuasive reason, but it won't be easy.

In addition, the leader will need the credibility to promise today actions in the future that sustain the benefit stream over time for costs incurred now. The further in the future these expected benefits are to arrive, the more important the credibility of the leader at this moment. The simple mathematics of compound interest (in this case, reversed) again explain why: It takes a remarkably modest discount rate to make *any benefits at all*, a hundred years from now, appear not worth the cost today. If there's no credibility around what we promise to do in the future, then the net present value of almost anything good in the reasonably far future comes perilously close to zero.

The leader will need embedded optimism. Not all societies and cultures share the peculiar trait of believing that the future can and will be better than the past. Americans do, and America is built on that belief. This can, and we hope will, become a self-fulfilling prophecy. At least to start, a society and culture that believes that the future will be better than the past has the right incentives to discount in ways that will plausibly make it so.

The challenge of articulating legitimate discount rates across a vast range of global concerns is probably the broadest issue that a foreign policy decision maker in America faces. One place where it comes together transparently will be in the U.S. approach to the future of international institutions. It's a good place to end this book, because it is so central to how Americans see their relationship to the world.

Notions of restorative leadership rest on the proposition that the international institutions the world needs have been handed down from the post–World War II generation, and that a United States which re-engages as a partner can tweak these institutions ever so gently toward the future. Moving from G-7 or G-8 (which had ceased to function as an economic management body of any significance some years ago) to G-20, and opening the possibility of the World Bank presidency to non-Americans and the International Monetary Fund managing directorship to non-Europeans are welcome changes. Yet these are initial steps more than transformative ones. They will only have lasting significance if they lead to rather than seek to substitute for more fundamental adaptations.

One truism of international relations theory is that it is harder, sometimes much harder, to create new international institutions than it is to sustain and modify existing ones. We believe that American foreign policy makers should now see that as an opportunity not a problem. It's an opportunity to signal our commitment to the future, our embedded optimism, and our reasoned calculation of discount rates that respects the mix of upside and downside risks we leave for future generations.

The next generation of international institutions needs to do more than simply increase the number of countries talking about currency stabilization, financial market reform, and capital adequacy ratios for banks. Those are important issues, but they are really just the starting point for the next phase of globalization.

The next phase of global leadership should prioritize issues that were essentially left out or left behind in a previous generation. The obvious issues include these: transnational crime and the deviant side of globalization, which includes the global trade in human organs, toxic waste, and slaves (for which "human trafficking" is a morally embarrassing euphemism). Carbon emissions, of course. Infectious and noninfectious disease (including tobacco-induced disease, and the induced lifestyle disease epidemic, now global, of obesity, hypertension, and diabetes). The flow of people (migration) and ideas (information and communications technologies and practices).

Some will say these are issues of secondary importance, their impact and threat to U.S. and global interests too far in the future to prioritize today when there are much more immediate threats like nuclear proliferation, terrorist plots, and banking crises. We say the fact that these issues are those whose importance rises in the future is exactly the point. Because a presumptive global leader should be leading that charge for investment.

It doesn't mean subtracting attention from today's immediate threats—that is always the starting point of statecraft and always will be. It means recognizing that dealing with those immediate threats is only the price of admission to the global game. It doesn't mean gainsaying the importance of traditional power in military and economic terms. It means acting in conjunction with the awareness that the competition among ideas is now the most uncertain dynamic in the broader contest for international leadership.

❧

Those twentieth-century five big ideas with which we began this book are no longer the sound and sturdy guides they once were. Although much about them still rings true, human and societal progress depend on adaptation to new realities. It's because the questions are both so big yet so open that the global competition of ideas is so important an ingredient of international politics—and such an uncertain one. That's why the challenge of leadership runs far deeper than the immediate issues of the day. The biggest, most basic questions about world order and just societies are open for debate.

Succeeding in this global competition of ideas requires letting go of Ptolemaic anachronisms (or aspirations) and recognizing the Copernican reality of international politics. It means visibly discarding assertions about what others must do because TINA says so. It means engaging the relentless competitive game that is the global marketplace of ideas as a full player but without presumptions of ownership or rule-making other than what is earned by the force of ideas and initiatives. It's when dominance gives way to influence that genuine leadership comes to the fore. The United States will be tested by global audiences in the next decade and beyond as never before. But so will every other contender for leadership in the competition of ideas. That leaves us optimistic. Because if Americans understand and embrace the terms of this new international game, there really is no one who can lead more effectively.

NOTES

1. BIG OPEN QUESTIONS

1. For example, Parag Khanna, *The Second World: Empires and Influence in the New Global Order* (New York: Random House, 2008); Paul Starobin, *After America: Narratives for the Next Global Age* (New York: Viking, 2008); Kishore Mahbubani, *The New Asian Hemisphere: The Irresistible Shift of Global Power to the East* (New York: Public Affairs, 2009).

2. German Marshall Fund survey of Europe, September 2009 (10 percent of Germans had a favorable opinion of G. W. Bush; 90 percent had a favorable view of Barack Obama).

3. See Charles Perrow, *Normal Accidents: Living with High Risk Technologies* (Princeton: Princeton University Press, 1984); Malcolm Gladwell, *The Tipping Point: How Little Things Can Make a Big Difference* (New York: Wheeler Publishing, 2003); Nassim Nicholas Taleb, *The Black Swan: The Impact of the Highly Improbable* (New York: Random House, 2007).

4. Edward Hallet Carr, *The Twenty Years Crisis 1919–1939: An In-*

troduction to the Study of International Relations (New York: Palgrave Macmillan, 1939).

5. Calvin Tomkins, "A Fool for Art: Onward and Upward with the Arts," *New Yorker* 83, 35 (November 2007), p. 65.

6. Andrew Kohut and Bruce Stokes, *America against the World: How We Are Different and Why We Are Disliked* (New York: Times Books, 2006), p. 35.

7. Hans Morgenthau, *Politics among Nations: The Struggle for Power and Peace* (New York: Alfred A. Knopf, 1948), p. 7.

2. A GLOBAL COMPETITION OF IDEAS

1. Joseph Nye, *Soft Power* (New York: Public Affairs, Perseus Books Groups), 2004.

2. Scott Wilson and Al Kamen, "Global War on Terror Is Given a New Name: Bush's Phrase Is Out, Pentagon Says," *Washington Post,* 25 March 2009.

3. Colin Powell, "US Forces: The Challenges Ahead," *Foreign Affairs,* Winter 1992; David H. Petraeus, et al., *The U.S. Army— Marine Corps Counterinsurgency Field Manual* (Chicago: University of Chicago Press, 2007).

4. In fact, the American academic international relations community helped (wittingly or unwittingly) to make this argument with its strong 1980s research agenda around "cooperation after hegemony."

5. Arthur M. Schlesinger, Jr., "Back to the Womb? Isolationism's Renewed Threat," *Foreign Affairs* 74:4 (July/August 1995), p. 4.

6. John Gerard Ruggie, *Multilateralism: The Theory and Praxis of an Institutional Form* (New York: Columbia University Press, 1993); John G. Ikenberry, "Getting Hegemony Right," *The National Interest,* 2001; Anne-Marie Slaughter, *The Idea that Is*

America: Keeping Faith with Our Values in a Dangerous World (New York: Basic Books, 2007).

7. Thomas Schelling, *The Strategy of Conflict* (Cambridge, MA: Harvard University Press, 1981).

8. Paul Krugman, "Competitiveness: A Dangerous Obsession," *Foreign Affairs,* March/April 1994.

9. "Text of President Bush's State of the Union Message," *New York Times,* 30 January 1991, p. A8.

10. Patrick E. Tyler, "U.S. Strategy Plan Calls for Insuring No Rivals Develop," *New York Times,* 8 March 1992.

11. Charles Krauthammer, "The Unipolar Moment," *Foreign Affairs* (America and the World), 1990.

12. Christopher A. Preble, *The Power Problem: How American Military Dominance Makes Us Less Safe, Less Prosperous and Less Free* (Ithaca: Cornell University Press, 2009), p. 5; Mark Danner, "Seeing the World: James Chace, 1931–2004," *New York Times Magazine,* 26 December 2004, http://www.markdanner.com/articles/print/29 [accessed 10 May 2010].

13. Condoleezza Rice, "Promoting the National Interest," *Foreign Affairs* 79:1 (January/February 2000), p. 47.

14. Alan Sipress, "Aggravated Allies Waiting for U.S. to Change Its Tune," *Washington Post,* April 22, 2001, p. A4; John R. Bolton, "Unilateralism Is Not Isolationism," in *Understanding Unilateralism in American Foreign Relations,* ed. Gwyn Prins (London: Royal Institute for International Affairs, 2000), p. 81.

15. "Stop the World, I Want to Get Off," *The Economist,* 28 July 2001.

16. Task Force on U.S. Standing in the World, "U.S. Standing in the World: Causes, Consequences and the Future," Peter J. Katzenstein and Jeffrey W. Legro, chairs (American Po-

litical Science Association, September 2009), https://www.apsanet.org/media/PDFs/APSA_TF_USStanding_Long_Report.pdf [accessed 10 May 2010].

17. President George W. Bush, *2002 National Security Strategy,* http://georgewbush-whitehouse.archives.gov/nsc/nss/2002/index.html [accessed 7 June 2010].

18. President Barack Obama, *2010 National Security Strategy,* http://www.whitehouse.gov/sites/default/files/rss_viewer/national_security_strategy.pdf [accessed 7 June 2010].

19. See, for example, Kristin Lord, *Voices of America: U.S. Public Diplomacy for the 21st Century* (Washington, DC: Brookings Institution, 2008).

20. Cass Sunstein, *Republic.com* (Princeton: Princeton University Press, 2001).

21. Jack A. Goldstone, "The New Population Bomb: The Four Megatrends That Will Change the World," *Foreign Affairs,* January/February 2010, pp. 31–33.

22. Goldstone, "The New Population Bomb," p. 38.

23. Joshua Cooper Ramo, *The Age of the Unthinkable: Why the New World Disorder Constantly Surprises Us and What We Can Do About It* (New York: Little, Brown, 2009), pp. 4, 181, 190.

24. George F. Kennan, *American Diplomacy: 1900–1950* (Chicago: University of Chicago Press, 1951).

25. Philip E. Tetlock, *Expert Political Judgment: How Good Is It? How Can We Know?* (Princeton: Princeton University Press, 2006).

26. Justice Oliver Wendell Holmes, dissenting, *Abrams et. al. v. United States,* 250 U.S. 630 (1919).

3. FORGING A JUST SOCIETY

1. Warren Hoge, "Latin America Losing Hope on Democracy," *New York Times,* 22 April 2004, p. A3.

2. Cited in George Perkovich, "Giving Justice Its Due," *Foreign Affairs* 84 (July/August 2005), p. 89.

3. Amartya Sen, *The Idea of Justice* (Cambridge, MA: Belknap Press, 2009).

4. Clinton Rossiter, ed., *The Federalist Papers* (New York: New American Library, 1961), p. 77.

5. John Rawls, *A Theory of Justice* (Cambridge, MA: Belknap Press, 1971).

6. Cited in Thomas Friedman, "Singapore and Katrina," *New York Times,* 14 September 2005.

7. Charles Perrow, *Normal Accidents: Living with High-Risk Technologies* (New York: Basic Books, 1984).

8. Joseph S. Nye, Jr., *The Paradox of American Power: Why the World's Only Superpower Can't Go It Alone* (Oxford: Oxford University Press, 2002), p. 9; Hans J. Morgenthau, cited in Michael J. Smith, "Ethics and Intervention," *Ethics and International Affairs* 3 (1989), p. 8.

9. Thomas Kuhn, *Structure of Scientific Revolutions* (Chicago: University of Chicago Press, 1982).

10. This argument, ironically, echoes E. H. Carr in *The Twenty Years' Crisis* (Oxford: Clarendon Press, 1939).

11. Joel L. Fleishman, *The Foundation: A Great American Secret* (New York: Public Affairs, 2007).

12. AsiaBarometer Survey Data, 2007. https://www.asiabarometer.org/en/data [accessed 15 March 2010].

4. PURSUING A TWENTY-FIRST-CENTURY WORLD ORDER

1. Thucydides, *History of the Peloponnesian War,* trans. R. Warner (New York: Penguin, 1972), p. 401.

2. Naazneen Barma, Ely Ratner, and Steve Weber, "A World Without the West," *The National Interest* 90 (July/August 2007), pp. 23–30.

3. Kenneth N. Waltz, *Theory of International Politics* (New York: McGraw-Hill, 1979).

4. Dennis Blair, testimony before the House Select Committee on Energy Independence and Global Warming, Oil Shock: Potential for Crisis Hearing, 7 November 2007, available at http://globalwarming.house.gov/tools/assets/files/0197.pdf [accessed 7 June 2010].

5. Clayton M. Christensen, *The Innovator's Dilemma* (Allston, MA: Harvard Business School Press, 1997), p. xviii.

6. There is an analogous argument about the medieval to modern transformation and the contemporary nation-state in John Ruggie, "Finding Our Feet in Territoriality: Problematizing Modernity in International Relations," *International Organization* 47 (Winter 1992), 139–175.

7. For example, John Mearsheimer, *The Tragedy of Great Power Politics* (New York: Norton, 2001).

8. Robert Jervis, "Cooperation Under the Security Dilemma," *World Politics*, 1978.

9. G. John Ikenberry, *After Victory: Institutions, Strategic Restraint and Rebuilding Order after Major Wars* (Princeton: Princeton University Press, 2001).

10. Cited in Jacob Heilbrunn, "An Officer and a Professor," *The National Interest* 92 (November/December 2007), p. 93.

11. The precise size and composition of China's foreign exchange reserves is not public, but estimates of U.S. Treasury debt as of early 2010 hover around 900 billion dollars.

12. Barma, Ratner, and Weber, "The World Without the West."

13. Robert Gilpin, *War and Change in World Politics* (Cambridge: Cambridge University Press, 1981).

14. Robert O. Keohane, "Reciprocity in International Relations," *International Organization*, 1986.

15. Robert Axelrod, *The Evolution of Cooperation* (Cambridge, MA: Basic Books, 1984).

16. Oliver Hart and John Moore, "Incomplete Contracts and Re-negotiation," *Econometrica* 56 (1988), 755-785 is an example.

17. Steven Weber, *The Success of Open Source* (Cambridge, MA: Harvard University Press, 2004).

18. Bruce W. Jentleson, "Tough Love Multilateralism," *The Washington Quarterly* (Winter 2003-04).

5. BEING STRATEGIC ABOUT THE FUTURE

1. Michael Porter, "What Is Strategy?" *Harvard Business Review*, November 1996.

2. This is, as it appears to be, a critique of at least some U.S. academic scholarship in this area.

3. http://www.vivario.org.br/publique/cgi/cgilua.exe/sys/start .htm?tpl=home [accessed 10 May 2010].

4. This is drawn from our New Era Global Scenarios Project, with the assistance of Naazneen Barma, Brent Durbin, and Ely Ratner.

5. Michael Barnett and Martha Finnemore, *Rules for the World: International Organizations in Global Politics* (Ithaca: Cornell University Press, 2004).

6. Edward C. Luck, *Mixed Messages: American Politics and International Organizations, 1919–1999* (Washington, D.C.: Brookings Institution Press, 1999).

7. Vaclav Havel, address to the U.S. Congress, 21 February 1990, cited in Bruce W. Jentleson, *American Foreign Policy: The Dynamics of Choice in the 21st Century* (New York: W.W. Norton, 2010), 4th ed., pp. 613, 96.

8. Cited in ibid., p. 91.

9. Michael Lewis, *The Big Short: Inside the Doomsday Machine* (New York: W.W. Norton, 2010).

Index

Abortion, 72–73
Affiliative sorting, 46–47
Afghanistan, 37–38, 110, 111
Agflation, 82, 120
Aguinaldo, Emilio, 180
Al-Qaeda, 23, 35, 44, 158, 161–162
Albright, Madeleine, 33
Altruism, 137–138
Amazon.com, 46
Anarchy, 88, 106, 107, 123, 139
Anti-Americanism, 56, 59–60, 116
Antitrust regulation, 76–77
Arab Peace Initiative, 38
Arrogance, 27, 68–69, 125–126
Artists, 21
Authority, 112; disruptive innovation and, 122–129
Automobile industry, 29–30
Autonomy, 70–75
Axelrod, Robert, 139

Basic human needs, 97
Bias, 47
Blair, Dennis, 111
Bono, 4
Boundary dissolution, 45–46
Brazil, 10
Building Resources Across Communities, 162
Bush, George H. W., 32–33
Bush, George W., 5, 13, 18–19, 33–34, 36–37, 58–59, 102, 126–127, 179
Business for Diplomatic Action, 40

Cairo speech, 57, 70
Capitalism, 1, 2, 4, 29–30, 61
Carbon capture and sequestration technology, 141–143
Carr, E. H., 7, 108
Cell biology, 129–130

Chace, James, 33

Chávez, Hugo, 179

Cheney, Dick, 32–33

China, 5, 10, 37, 71–72, 102; dollar holdings of, 132, 133–134, 152; just society leadership proposition of, 88–91; U.S. relationship with, 174–175, 181–182

Christensen, Clayton, 112–113

Churchill, Winston, 39

Cities, developing-world, 48–51

Civil rights, 84

Climate change, 141–143, 170, 189–191

Clinton, William, 33, 167

Cold War, 10, 23, 28, 124, 151

Common interests, 169–170

Competitiveness, 30–32; borderless nature of, 56–60; demography and, 48–51; digital infrastructure and, 43–48; geopolitical, 32–37; innovation in, 35–36; for just society, 84–95; market characteristics of, 51–58; Paul Krugman on, 31

Consensus, 46–47

Consistency, 24

Constant Gardener, The (Le Carré), 41

Containment, 28, 124

Cooperation, 139–140

Copenhagen Climate Conference, 190–191

Copernican world, 10–11, 35, 52–53, 195; versus Ptolemaic world, 9–10, 195

Copernicus, 10

Council on Competitiveness, 31

Credibility, 191–192

Culture, American, 1, 2, 5, 50, 61

Culture wars, 21

Declinists, 15

Decolonization, 28, 103, 124

Deepwater Horizon oil spill, 82–83

Defense-dominance, 120–121

Defense Policy Guidance, of George H. W. Bush, 32–33

Democracy, 1, 2, 4–5, 67–68; alternative -isms to, 175–184; interventionism and, 181–182; promotion of, 180–181

Demography, global, 48–51

Denmark, 85–86

Deterrence, 17, 18, 20, 113, 151

Dictatorship, 68

Diffuse reciprocity, 139–140

Digital infrastructure, 43–48

Diplomacy, 39–40

Discounting, 186–192

Disruptive innovation, 114–131; authority and, 122–129; power and, 117–122; resiliency and, 129–131

Dissuasion, 17, 18

Doha Round trade negotiations, 127, 143–144

Dollar, value of, 132–134

Dominance, 55–56, 118, 120–121

Domino theory, 108

Drugs: availability of, 98–99; clinical trials for, 41–42

Effectiveness, 112

Eisenhower, Dwight, 84

Elections, 74, 76, 126–127

Energy, 4, 141–143, 189–190

Escalation, ideological, 23

Euro, value of, 133

European Union, 10

Evolution of Cooperation, The (Axelrod), 139

Failed states, 131, 160

Federalist Papers, The (Madison), 78–79

Finance, 4, 28; global crisis (2008–2009) in, 109–110, 121–122, 128–129, 132–133, 183–184

Gates Foundation, 4, 91–92, 159, 161

Gazprom, 159

Genocide Convention (1948), 127

Global gag rule, 72–73

Globalization, 10–11, 54–55, 77–78

Google, 4

Gore, Al, 190

Gulf War, 32

Halliburton, 159

Hamas, 72, 159

Havel, Vaclav, 125, 179–180

Hegemony, American, 1–2, 3–4, 26–28, 52–53, 61

Heterogeneity, 83–84

Hezbollah, 54, 72, 94–95, 159

HIV/AIDS, 98

Holmes, Oliver Wendell, 60

Homeostasis, 129–130

Howard, Sir Michael, 124

Hull, Cordell, 127

Humphreys, David, 180

Hurricane Katrina, 79–81

Hypocrisy, 21–22, 125

IBM, 10, 159

Idea of Justice, The (Sen), 72

Ideology (ideologies), 6–8; borders and, 56–60; competition among, 12–16, 18–24, 36–40, 51–58; end of, 7–8, 53; escalation and, 23; global demography and, 48–51; global digital infrastructure and, 43–48; universal applicability of, 86–87; war of, 18–20, 22–23

Ikenberry, John, 27, 124

Image vs. text, 44–45, 50

Immigration, 65, 83–84

Income inequality, 78

Inconvenient Truth, An (Gore), 190

India, 10

Individualism vs. individuality, 71

Industrial Revolution, 189

Industry: agriculture, 82, 120, 144; automobile, 29–30; energy, 4, 141–143; finance, 4, 28; monopolies in, 76–77; pharmaceutical, 41–42, 98–99; technology, 10, 54–55

Innovation, 112–117; disruptive, 114–131; sustaining, 112–113

Intellectual property policy, 97–99

Internet, 43–48, 56–57, 73

Interventionism, 181–182

Invincibility, loss of, 150-154
Iran, 152
Iraq War, 34-35, 37, 110, 111
Isolationism, 25-26
Israel, 153

Japan, 29-30
Jefferson, Thomas, 57, 75
Jervis, Robert, 120
Just society, 62-64; autonomy and, 70-75; Chinese leadership proposition and, 88-91; communications technology and, 94; competition for, 84-95; definition of, 63-64; flawed assumptions about, 68-70; formulas for, 66-67; geographical security and, 65-66; heterogeneity and, 83-84; intellectual property policy and, 97-99; legitimacy and, 95-100; material abundance and, 65, 66; nongovernmental organizations and, 91-95; opportunity and, 75-79; process vs. outcome and, 67-68; protection and, 79-83; religious movements and, 94-95
Justice, 96-97

Kennan, George, 26, 55-56
Korean War, 26
Krauthammer, Charles, 33
Krugman, Paul, 31
Kyoto treaty, 34

Le Carré, John, 41
Leadership: adaptive vs. restor-ative, 13, 63, 192-193; authority and, 112, 122-129; autonomy and, 70-75; challenge of, 2-3; competition for, 24-25, 131-137; component characteristics of, 111-112; comprehensiveness and, 87; consistent, 24; credibility and, 191-192; disruptive innovation and, 114-131; effectiveness and, 112; equilibrium end-state claim of, 87-88; heterogeneity and, 83-84; hypocrisy and, 21-22; incremental corrosion of, 134-135; innovation and, 112-117; justice and, 96-97, 99-100 (see also Just society); legitimacy and, 95-100; market, 24-25; mutuality and, 104-105, 137-146; opportunity and, 75-79; optimism and, 192; overpromise/underdeliver and, 125-128; power and, 117-122; presumptive, 24; preventive action and, 191-192; priorities for, 193-194; protection and, 79-83, 144-145; renewal of, 38; transparent, 24; twenty-first century world order and, 106-111; unilateralism vs. multilateralism and, 170-175; universal applicability and, 86-87; vision and, 112
Legitimacy, 8, 95-100, 123-125
Libby, Lewis "Scooter," 33
Lincoln, Abraham, 180
Lippmann, Walter, 55
Luck, Edward, 173
Ludlow amendment, 26

Madison, James, 78–79

Magaziner, Ira, 30

Medical biological materials, Russian export of, 41–42

Megaphilanthropies, 91–95, 158–166

Mill, John Stuart, 23

Monopolies, 76–77

Monroe Doctrine, 25

Morgenthau, Hans, 15, 26, 84

Multilateralism, 104–105, 145–146, 169–175

Mutuality, 38, 104–105, 137–146; definition of, 140

National Security Strategy Document, 36–37, 38

Natsios, Andrew, 165

Nongovernmental organizations, 91–95, 158–166; central roles of, 163–166; expansion of, 162–163; U.S. policy toward, 164–166

North American Free Trade Agreement, 113

Nye, Joseph, 84

Obama, Barack, 5, 37, 38, 59, 102, 126, 167, 180–181; Cairo speech of, 57, 70

Offense-dominance, 120–121

Opportunity, 75–79

Optimism, 192

Overpromise/underdeliver, 125–128

Pax Americana, 109

Peace, 1, 3, 61; vs. world order, 107–108

Pearl Harbor, 65

Philanthrophy, global, 91–95, 158–166

Philippines, 180

Piracy, 119

Politics, 7–8

Population, global, 48–51

Populism, 175–184

Post-American world, 2

Power, 7, 8–9, 15; disruptive innovation and, 117–122; economic, 9, 10; G. W. Bush on, 33–34; global systems of, 11–13; hard, 17–18; ideological, 9; impenetrable concentration of, 75–77; military, 9, 10, 110–111, 120–121, 164; of nonstate actors, 161; soft, 17, 18, 43, 58, 84; unipolar, 32–35

Power-influence gap, 102

Pre-emption, 20

Preventive action, 184–192

Protection, 79–83, 144–145

Ptolemy, 9–10

Public diplomacy, 39–40

Public discourse, 20–21, 22, 57–58

Public goods, 169–170, 174

Putin, Vladimir, 93

Ramo, Joshua Cooper, 54

Rand, Ayn, 71

Rational actor model, 42

Reagan, Ronald, 29, 153

Reciprocity, 138–140; diffuse, 139–140

Reich, Robert, 30

Religious movements, 94–95

Renminbi, 133, 134

Republic.com (Sunstein), 46

Resiliency, disruptive innovation and, 129–131

Roosevelt, Franklin D., 26

Ruggie, John, 27

Rumsfeld, Donald, 17

Russia, 10, 93, 152

Russian Federal Customs Service, 41–42

Schelling, Thomas, 28, 35–36

Schlesinger, Arthur, Jr., 26

Sen, Amartya, 72

Singapore, 86

Slaughter, Anne-Marie, 27

Smoot-Hawley Tariff Act, 25

Social democracy, 85–86

South Africa, 98

Stability, 108–109

State determination, 175–184

Status quo, 108–109, 153

Stein, Janice, 68–69

Strategic action, 153–158; cooperation and, 157; definition of, 153–154; democracy and, 175–184; future problems and, 184–192; goal of, 155; nonstate actors and, 158–166; preventive, 184–192; uncertainty and, 155–156; unilateral/multilateral, 166–175; vs. weakness, 156–157

Strategy of Conflict, The (Schelling), 28

Structural Impediments Initiative, 30

Sunstein, Cass, 46

Sweden, 85–86

Systems: collapse of, 6–7; disruption of, 119–122

Terrorism, American response to, 17–18

Thucydides, 101–102

Thurow, Lester, 30–31

TINA, 11–12, 24, 62, 131, 133, 147, 195; versus THEMBA, 12, 171

Transparency, 24

Triumphalism, 125–126

Twenty Years Crisis, The (Carr), 7, 108

Uncertainty, 155–156, 181–182; discounting and, 186–192

Unilateralism, 33–35, 166–168, 170

United Nations, 127

Universal Declaration of Human Rights, 127

Values, American, 39, 56–57

Vargas Llosa, Mario, 68

Venezuela, 152

Venture capitalists, 21

Violence, legitimate monopoly on, 53–54

Vision, 112, 146–147

Viva Rio, 162

Voluntary Export Restrictions, 29

Walesa, Lech, 125

War, 3, 107–108; metaphor of, 12, 19–20

Weakness, 152–153, 156–157

Westphalian sovereignty, 53–54

Wilson, Woodrow, 180

Wolfowitz, Paul, 33

"World Competitiveness Report," 29

World Health Organization, 165–166

World order: alternative -isms and, 175–184; authority and, 122–129; definition of, 106–111; disruptive innovation and, 114–131; hegemonic, 1–2, 3–4, 26–28, 52–53, 61; historical perspective on, 101–104; innovation and, 112–117; leadership proposition about, 106–111; mutuality and, 104–105, 137–146; power and, 117–122; resiliency and, 129–131; systems disruption and, 119–122; transactional, 135–137; unilateralism vs. multilateralism and, 170–175; vision and, 146–147; vs. *Pax Americana,* 109; vs. peace, 107–108; vs. stability, 108–109; "without the West," 135–137. *See also* Leadership

World Trade Center attack, 65, 119

World War II, 26, 103

World Wide Web, 44

Yoo, John, 44

YouTube, 44, 159